BOUND
TOGETHER

BOUND TOGETHER

A Theology for
Ecumenical Community Ministry

A. DAVID BOS

THE
PILGRIM
PRESS
Cleveland

To Johanna

The Pilgrim Press, 700 Prospect Avenue
Cleveland, Ohio 44115, U.S.A.
thepilgrimpress.com

© 2005 by The Pilgrim Press

Printed in the United States of America on acid-free paper

10 09 08 07 06 05   5 4 3 2 1

Library of Congress Cataloging-in-Publication Data
Bos, A. David.
   Bound together : a theology for ecumenical community ministry /
A. David Bos.
      p.   cm.
   Includes bibliographical references (p.   ) and index.
   ISBN 0-8298-1628-3 (paper: alk. paper)
   1. Church work. 2. Pastoral theology. 3. Interdenominational
cooperation. I. Title.
BV4400.B636 2005
280'.042 – dc22

                                             2004065049

Contents

Foreword

None but the isolated can miss the assault on local communities that issues from the downside of economic globalization. It is not new, however, but a steady fact of accelerated change in modern industrial and postindustrial society.

Faith communities have been deeply affected, and many have responded. A striking sector of that response is the ecumenical and interfaith community ministry engaged in cutting-edge, but little-noticed, work since the 1960s. This ministry is markedly local in organization and orientation, with neighborhood crises often the precipitating cause and neighborhood issues the focus. Coalitions and achievements have been remarkable, and frustrations and broken relationships numerous.

A how-to literature focused on the organization and practice of community ministry exists. David Bos, the author of this volume and himself a longtime professional in the field, wrote one of those: *A Practical Guide to Community Ministry* (1993).

A literature of local narratives and personal spiritual journeys amidst specific ministries also exists, much of it deeply moving and instructive. Heidi Neumark's *Breathing Space: A Spiritual Journey in the South Bronx* (2003) is one such account.

Yet, oddly, no substantial theology of ecumenical and interfaith community ministry exists, except in the most general terms. No account, to my knowledge, has asked

whether a working theology may not already be present
in these joint endeavors, perhaps on the basis of an "embedded unity" (Bos's phrase) that already exists by virtue
of active investment in a shared neighborhood. None has
drawn comparisons of this manner of ministry and its working theology to better-known theological currents discussed
in other circles, such as seminaries and universities. Nor
has the sort of important ecumenical and interfaith work
done here been well compared with work in other venues
of ecumenical and interfaith exchange. Finally, the number
of constructive, comprehensive theological proposals offered
from within the experience of community ministry is very
limited. Bos's "broken covenant" and its repair is one of very
few. Community theology as offered here has been largely
missing-in-action.

The title, *Bound Together: A Theology for Ecumenical
Community Ministry*, is precise. This is a theology both
born of and offered for community ministry done in a manner utterly necessary now — namely, on an ecumenical/
interfaith basis. As such it sometimes clarifies and en-
ergizes an embedded rationale already in place, but left
inarticulate. Other times it helps create the very hope and
direction needed for faith-based neighborhood transformation. "Bound Together" is itself a rich, shared theological
theme, given that all religions make the rather astounding
claim that we are born to belonging in creation understood as nothing less than a cosmic community. At the
same time, Bos uses "covenant" to deepen the theology
of being "bound together." Covenant, of course, is utterly
biblical for Jews, Christians, and Muslims. Their forma-
tive stories are stories of the making, breaking, and repair
of covenants. These are "Peoples of the Way," where "the
Way" is often cast as a covenant. But "covenant" is also
richly public as an image for society as citizens "bound together." Here, too, making, breaking, and repairing pertain.
Bos himself is obviously at home here, theologically and

from decades of experience in ministry, as he moves with fine ease between local faith communities and society in terms of shared bonds. The assault on local communities will continue. So will dogged and creative responses. With these pages, and to our benefit, Bos has offered his contribution.

LARRY L. RASMUSSEN

Reinhold Niebuhr Professor Emeritus of Social Ethics
Union Theological Seminary, New York City

Preface

It has been my good fortune to reside in Louisville, Kentucky, where excellent practitioners of community ministry abound in all the neighborhoods of the metropolitan area — persons who have given me so much encouragement and inspiration for the writing of this book. I am indebted also to friends in the Interfaith Community Ministry Network (1983–2003), where, through the years in regional and national consultations, hundreds of community ministries from every region of the country shared their experience and wisdom.

As a result of conversations with such persons and in the light of my own professional experience in directing community ministries, I became convinced that a theological approach to the subject was a necessary augmentation to earlier, strictly practical works, including my own *A Practical Guide to Community Ministry* (1993). I began the project with a research grant from the Lilly Endowment; the periodic advice and consultation of Professor Larry Rasmussen of Union Theological Seminary (New York), for which I am most grateful, saw me through to the end. I wish to thank the administration and staff of the library of Louisville Presbyterian Theological Seminary for their friendly and helpful responses to my every request.

At the completion of the first draft, I had the privilege of hosting a symposium on the subject, which served as basis for later revisions. Participants in that symposium, which

was held in the rooms of Auburn Theological Seminary
(at Union Seminary), included Larry Rasmussen, Rein-
hold Niebuhr Professor of Social Ethics; Dale P. Andrews,
Associate Professor of Homiletics and Pastoral Theology,
Louisville Presbyterian Theological Seminary; Sue Culver,
Executive Secretary, Bradford, England Inner Ring Group;
David Leslie, Executive Director, Ecumenical Ministries of
Oregon; Isabel Morrison, Social Action Coordinator (Re-
tired), Downtown United Presbyterian Church, Rochester,
New York; Margaret Thomas, Interim Coordinator for Inter-
faith Relations, Presbyterian Church (USA); and Johanna
van Wijk-Bos, Dora Pierce Professor of Bible, Louisville
Presbyterian Theological Seminary. I thank them for their
insightful critiques and suggestions.

I especially wish to think my wife, Johanna, for her in-
valuable assistance in editing and revising the manuscript
as it progressed from draft to draft.

Thanks also to Ulrike Guthrie of The Pilgrim Press for
her sympathetic shepherding of the book to publication.

Introduction

Is your congregation searching for a way to relate more effectively to its surrounding neighborhood, to break out from its cocoon of many years, to link to other congregations and institutions for the building of community? A theology of community ministry provides a mandate for such a transformation. Are you engaged with a community ministry where the relationships have grown stale, programs and activities partake of sameness from year to year, and the avenues of progressive change seem to be blocked? A theology of community ministry opens the way to a heightened appreciation of the significance of any community, its possibilities, its assets and needs, its strengths and vulnerabilities. Do you wonder how a community, with its variety of religious groupings, can or should respond to the economic pressures of globalization and the impersonal impact of megainstitutions; to the reality of decision-makers in distant boardrooms who, willy-nilly, determine the fate of a neighborhood; to the cynicism and passivity that permeates the citizenry? A theology of community ministry will be an antidote to these and other dilemmas that threaten the God-given fabric of responsible relationships in the place where you live. This theology intends to be a sign of hope for congregations, clusters of congregations, and their communities in a variety of circumstances.

"Community ministry" refers to a concrete interfaith and ecumenical movement that sprang to life in the mid-1960s in various locations throughout the United States and Canada. In some areas now, these clusters are so numerous and so much a fixture in the community that they are almost taken for granted. The movement has its echoes in other countries as well. In the United Kingdom these projects are called "Local Ecumenical Partnerships" (LEPs) when they have the approbation of denominational leaders. In the Netherlands they go under the rubric of "Kerk en Buurt" (Church and Neighborhood). In almost all cases in the United States and elsewhere these projects involve various degrees of cooperation or integration of congregations of different denominations and/or faiths, the focus of which is the surrounding community.

I believe that the most vital and significant interfaith/ ecumenical activity is found in local communities. Even in this age of recrudescent fundamentalisms, real and visible progress in ecumenical and interfaith relations is being made at this level throughout the world. Since the September 11, 2001, attacks, interfaith relations have become a priority in many places. A diversity of religious expression and increasing interreligious contacts may now be observed even in nonmetropolitan communities. Theological reflection on the specifically local aspect of these developments is appropriate and overdue.

In this book I argue that local communities are the most likely, most hopeful, and most needful points of departure toward the renewal of a torn or "broken covenant," which heretofore has sustained society understood as a polis or political entity. I maintain that local congregations, when they work together across denominational and faith boundaries, may play a critical role in this rehabilitative task.

In reply to the objection that "local" is susceptible to relativization to the point of meaninglessness, I have in mind qualitative and quantitative parameters that define the term. First, communities may be counted upon to define themselves as "local" by several possible indices, most of which involve a degree of personal interaction. Second, I use a rule of thumb of twenty thousand to fifty thousand inhabitants that compose an urban neighborhood, suburban area, small city, or rural county. I derive these limits mainly from my experience as an executive of community ministry organizations in three of the above types of communities. I believe these parameters will withstand scrutiny based on the academic canons of sociology, economics, and political science, though I cannot claim expertise in these fields.

The reference to Robert Bellah's work in the title reflects a basic agreement with his thesis that one finds in American history in particular an implicit kind of master narrative that is epitomized by the religio-political term "covenant." Scholars in several disparate fields have made this discovery before and after Bellah — including the theologian Richard Niebuhr, the historian Perry Miller, and the political scientist Daniel Elazar. Whether or not one speaks of a civil religion in this regard, it is quite possible to speak of a political fabric with a specific transcendent reference that through the years has brought coherence and promise to the American experiment.

To be sure, "covenant" carries historical baggage. Eric Mount describes both its current liabilities and utility.[1] Yet recent biblical scholarship increasingly recognizes a universal dimension in the primordial concept of covenant in the Hebrew Bible. I am persuaded that where covenant is employed to justify rank exclusivism (as in the apartheid regime of South Africa or in today's gated North American communities), this is a misappropriation of the word that does not stand the tests of historical and exegetical analysis. I refer the reader to an excellent study by Norbert Lohfink and Erich Zenger.[2] The authors maintain that although the covenant is a prerogative of Israel and grounded in the election of Israel by God, it always had an ultimate relevance and reference to the nations of the world and "threaded through the entire fabric of the Hebrew Bible, was already wound unto the spool in Gen. 12:1–3."[3] Mount argues the contemporary relevance of covenant even when it is not made to depend upon the biblical roots. He says that the *difference* of the other makes covenant possible and to the extent that it elicits compassion and obligation, it is necessary. "It points us to the unavoidable sphere of the interhuman and the need for mutuality, empathy and dialogue."[4] In my opinion, these and other works, including the magisterial multivolume work by Daniel Elazar, establish the relevance of the term in our common life for some time to come.[5]

There has never been a "golden age" of the covenant in America. The famous sermon by John Winthrop, referred to in this book and by countless others, was compromised by Winthrop himself in his banishment of Anne Hutchinson from the Massachusetts Bay Colony. Like the idea of America itself, its reference has always been to a future just beyond the present's reach. Have ever its "alabaster cities gleamed undimmed by human tears"? We cannot in any sense speak of the covenant as a historical achievement. It is rather a mutual promise that, even when seemingly broken, lends meaning and cohesion to our common life. As such I hope to show that it displays a fitting, normative vision for interfaith and ecumenical community ministry in building and defending local community.

Chapter 1

The Congregations

Their Embedded Unity

We begin with a typical community ministry dilemma: Let us suppose that several Christian congregations covenant to institute and incorporate a community ministry with a budget, a staff, a representative board, and stated social mission goals. Suppose the board decides to extend an invitation to a Jewish congregation to become a part of the organization. One of the Christian congregations, objecting to this invitation, quits the community ministry, withdrawing its financial and volunteer support. This is a scenario that gets played out frequently in many variations — Christian congregations making their participation in community ministry contingent upon the exclusion of other faith groups or, sometimes, other Christian denominations. Questions arise: Is the withdrawing congregation justified without at least considering the possibility that it might be violating a prior, God-given relationship that involves certain obligations to the other congregations, including the Jewish one? Is the congregation that withdraws merely terminating a relationship, into which it voluntarily entered in the first place, which has no basis other than that voluntary decision? Or is it attempting to end a relationship that, at one level, cannot be dissolved?

Or, take the case of an urban community ministry that numbers among its membership several "nonecumenical" congregations — congregations of faith groups or denominations that are, in principle, opposed to becoming part of certain larger ecumenical or interfaith groupings. This community ministry refuses to join a metropolitan ecumenical and interfaith organization out of deference to its "nonecumenical" congregations, which have probably already strained internal relations by joining the community ministry. Is the community ministry justified in not joining the larger circle of cooperation? Or is it merely acknowledging the theological priority of relationships at the most local level?

The fundamental relationship of an ecumenical or interfaith community ministry is with the congregations that God has joined together to act on behalf of their community. So how is the relationship among participating congregations in this ministry to be understood theologically? And is there a given theological relationship among the congregations of a neighborhood? When congregations decide to engage in social mission jointly, are they merely recognizing each other's existence and establishing a relationship based solely on a common undertaking? Or are they building on a preexistent, given theological relationship? More to the point, are they choosing to establish a relationship, which presumably they might also dissolve if for some reason their joint project in community ministry were to be discontinued? Or are they bound together in a theological relationship in any case?

These questions raise another: is it responsible for any congregation of any faith to behave toward its neighboring congregations as if they did not exist or as if they had nothing to do with each other? The reality is, of course, that many congregations behave in precisely this insouciant way. My contention is that there can be no theological justification for it, and that ecumenical/interfaith community ministry builds on sinking sand whenever it defines itself apart from, or ignores this theological issue of why and how congregations in a given area are related.

Congregations of a neighborhood or small town or county are tied to each other in many ways — by the culture of the area, by socioeconomic structures, and by family and other personal relationships. Gary Gunderson compares congregations in their community to a forest where the roots of the trees form an interwoven fabric.[1] But a congregation, unlike a tree, may choose to ignore the "deeply woven roots." It might disentangle itself more or less successfully from all ties. It might take pride in its ability to stand alone — a tree thriving apart from the forest. But its solitary strategy cannot be supported theologically if, implicit in its identity as a community of faith, there is a covenant relationship with other congregations of the neighborhood.

It is not uncommon to hear persons argue for the formation of local coalitions of congregations based on the logic of efficiency and economy. (I have often argued the case in this way.) We sell ecumenical and interfaith community ministry short with this argument. A congregation with plenty of resources will not be persuaded by the argument from efficiency, nor should it be. Congregations must be confronted with the reality of a relatedness, which cannot responsibly be ignored.

George Webber, a founder of the East Harlem Protestant Parish, a precursor of the modern community ministry movement, wrote that his goal was to see that "Ordinary congregations are vehicles through which men [sic] may discover the reality of Christian life and be equipped to live with integrity, with coherence between what they profess as Christians and the reality of their life in the world and in the church."[2] For George Webber, it was obvious that the realization of this goal depended upon an ecumenical (if not also interfaith) context for ministry. In observing that the

Inner City Protestant Parish in Cleveland, the West Side Christian Parish in Chicago, and his East Harlem Protestant Parish were special ministries created where there was a vacuum, he noted, "The existing congregations of an inner city neighborhood must also learn to work in unity."[3]

Webber anticipated the community ministry movement. He did not realize, probably, that the movement would arise not just in the inner cities, where the pressure of human need would overcome denominational differences, but also in towns, rural counties, and suburbs. He did, however, take pains to note that this banding together of congregations would have theological/biblical roots as well as strategic and pragmatic virtues. Webber fashioned a kind of theological platform for community ministry using the biblical concept of covenant. He thought that Christian scriptures were best understood in terms of covenant, and that studying the scriptures rightly will make this concept come alive in the community of the faithful, across denominational lines, for the benefit of the larger community.[4]

Embedded Unity Historically Viewed

Every now and then we hear echoes of an earlier day, when any congregation was assumed to be an ecumenical and/or interfaith entity. In one case, a fire destroyed the buildings of the largest member congregation in the community ministry. (With a membership numbering several thousand it was one of the most aggressive in recruiting members from other congregations!) Within hours after the fire, every one of that congregation's numerous programs and activities found accommodations in the buildings of the nearby congregations. Such a response is faithful. It seemed a matter of course. The faithfulness of the response reflected the embedded, covenantal, theological relationship of which we are speaking.

As American villages were settled during the seventeenth, eighteenth, and nineteenth centuries, congregations shared buildings, preachers, and members. They joined in revivals — as well as patriotic and other civic occasions — and they participated in each other's anniversaries and special events. If there was a local synagogue, it was not unusual for that congregation to be a part of this common religious life.[5] In other words, for the most part, the congregations acted as if there was a given connection among them to which they had to be faithful and for which they were responsible.

As cracks appeared in the structure of mainline Protestant hegemony in the early nineteenth century, basic elements of that legacy gradually fell into disrepute. In time, the congregation as institution, along with its embedded relationships with other congregations and along with Protestant piety, was fair game for every aspiring intellectual and social critic. Eventually, by the 1960s, for many graduating classes of theological seminaries, to become pastor of a congregation was considered one of the least attractive of available options.

In the mid-1970s a trend arose to rehabilitate this institution, the congregation, along with the pastoral office, the sermon, the centrality of scripture, and the theological enterprise, as well as individual and collective ways of prayer and meditation. This reappraisal extended into Catholic and non-Christian circles, with the result that the institution of the congregation is probably more entrenched as a part of local community life today than it was before the period of skepticism.

One part of this picture which has not been restored to its former place of respectability is the assumption that the congregation, by its very nature as a part of the local community, is an ecumenical and interfaith institution — that it has, ipso facto, operative ecumenical and interfaith ties. Part of our task in ecumenical and interfaith community ministry today is to complete the reappraisal and rehabilitation of the congregation by making this relational dimension more explicit.

The Significance of Embedded Unity: Congregations Compose the Foundation of Community Ministry

Community ministry often springs from a critical need that arises in the area. A Louisville, Kentucky, ministry started as a result of a devastating tornado that struck that neighborhood in 1974. More recently the spring floods experienced by many Midwestern towns have resulted in the organization of ongoing ecumenical and interfaith disaster-response ministries. These dramatic beginnings illustrate the crucial role that congregations acting collaboratively play in the life of any given community. Other less dramatic start-ups were based on a prehistory of congregations working together in specific ways on behalf of the wider community. The formation of such ecumenical/interfaith community ministries may have pointed the way toward a general theological and intellectual rehabilitation of the congregation as an institution.

Throughout the cultural and political upheavals of the 1960s, the congregation, no less than a host of other institutions, was under fire. The theological expression of this upheaval was the "kenotic" theology of the World Council of Churches, Hans Hoekendijk, Steve Rose, Gibson Winter, and others. "Kenotic" derives from the Greek word *kenosis* and indicates emptying, as in "Christ emptied himself, taking the form of a servant" (Phil. 2:7). This theology tended to advocate the forming of alternative "experimental ministries," which, rather than being seen as extensions of or supports for congregations, represented an implicit root-and-branch critique of the institution. Kenotic theology challenged the Christian church in general and local congregations specifically to "empty themselves" for the sake of the world in favor of other, aborning local vehicles of mission.

Ironically, one such experimental ministry came to be predicated on the existence and strengthening of congregations as constitutive units of social mission. George Webber of the East Harlem Protestant Parish (mentioned earlier) and Elizabeth O'Connor of the Church of the Saviour (see below) deemed the congregation a worthy, if impaired, institution for responding to the changing scene of the 1960s. In contrast to the kenotic theologians, they placed more emphasis on the institutional continuity that the congregation afforded. As such they became precursors of the community ministry movement.

Some years after the rise of community ministry, an academic movement, which became known as "congregational studies," appeared in a symbiotic and supportive role. These studies compose a monument to the endurance of the congregation as a local institution. Community ministry benefited from congregational studies because it strengthened respect for its key component. From experience, community ministry knew what was to be articulated in congregational studies: that each congregation possessed its own narrative, its own myth, and its own language, which were related as much or more to the locality of the congregation than its denominational affiliation. Thus, congregational studies clarified some of the dynamics of community ministry for its practitioners.

The classic work in the congregational studies literature is James Hopewell's *Congregation*. Eventually, Hopewell, in drawing on the work of Northrop Frye and his theory of literary structure, concluded, "Congregational culture is not an accidental accumulation of symbolic elements but a coherent system whose structured logic is narrative."[6] Hopewell's discovery of narrative as a vehicle of uniqueness — the story that the congregation tells itself about itself — gives us an important clue as to how to make explicit the unity among faith communities that we contend is embedded in the situation. Each congregation's story about its beginnings reveals its own perspective on the local community and, indirectly, on the other congregations. Perhaps one congregation began as a spin-off from another, either acrimoniously or amicably. Perhaps it met for a while in a building of another congregation. Perhaps it bought its building from a congregation. Perhaps it has a mandated relationship to a congregation of another denomination by virtue of interdenominational agreements at regional or national levels. A number of scenarios could be imagined — all demonstrating the given quality of the relationships. In ecumenical/interfaith community ministry we build, sometimes unaware, upon existing intercongregational narratives.

Finally, because congregations, according to Hopewell, attract to their fellowship those who want to participate in the unique local drama enacted there, each congregation, to a greater or lesser degree, encapsulates an "over and against" aspect vis-à-vis the wider community. That is, its story contains elements of tension or counterpoint relative to the story of the town, county, or neighborhood. Therefore, each congregational narrative may be seen as a kind of subplot of the larger local narrative. One might even find a theology — a civil theology perhaps — embedded in the story of the local settlement. If this were the case, such a theology would conform to the presuppositions of classical covenant theology, which embraces the civil and religious communities; it would also contribute to an understanding of community ministry as a theological relationship on behalf of the wider community. In other words, the various "unique local dramas" imply some kind of accommodation among them, and between them and the community at large.

These gleanings from a reading of Hopewell demonstrate how well he succeeded in showing that the "the thick gathering that is congregational life is more substantial than is usually acknowledged." (We would say that, by extension, the relationships among congregations are likewise more substantial.)[7]

Community Ministry as an Expression of Embedded Unity among Local Congregations

Some community ministries began as a declaration of hope and unity on the part of local congregations in an otherwise apparently fragmented society. This was the case with Smith Haven Ministries (later renamed The Ministries) in Suffolk County, Long Island. Founded in 1967 as the Nesconset Experimental Ministry, this was one of the grandparents of the movement. This ministry developed on the fast-growing and chaotic fringes of metropolitan New York and chose as its initial site the then-largest regional shopping mall in the United States — the only other unifying element in that area.

The first community ministries and their precursors — the East Harlem Protestant Parish and the Church of the Saviour — all respected the congregation at the same time as they responded to the longing for a different kind of congregation. Dietrich Bonhoeffer's influential book *Life Together* appeared in English in 1954. His concept of "religionless" Christianity mirrored the desire of many at the time to dispense with the trappings and get to the experience and the core of Christian community. Bonhoeffer attacked the superfluities in the Christian congregations in Germany in a time of ascendant Nazism, and he spoke disparagingly of "the clamorous desire for something more."[8]

Bonhoeffer's plea for a truly Christ-centered community of believers made a powerful impression on North American Christians — not only because it came from the pen of the most famous of those martyred in the anti-Nazi resistance, but also because it appeared at a time of enormous growth in size and numbers of congregations. This religious boom involved intense competition among the denominations in the burgeoning suburbs to which their members were fleeing from urban neighborhoods. Within radii of one or two miles on the outskirts of all the major cities, one could tour the "first units" of competing, homogeneous congregations. To many these congregations were founding themselves on "something more" than God as revealed in Christ.

Into this theologically ambiguous situation sounded Bonhoeffer's words: "Life together under the Word will remain sound and healthy only... where it shares actively and passively in the sufferings, and struggles and promise of the whole Church.... The exclusion of the weak and insignificant, the seemingly useless people,... may actually mean the exclusion of Christ; in the poor brother Christ is knocking at the door."[9] Oneness in Christ was the only legitimate basis for Christian community; all purely human foundations were tantamount to rejecting Christ. These words fed both the kenotic, anti-institutional stream and the hope for a different kind of congregation.

Enter the Church of the Saviour in Washington, D.C. This congregation sprang partly from the desire to shape itself into the kind of community for which Bonhoeffer called. Elizabeth O'Connor began her description of this congregation with the same text from Psalm 133:1 with which Bonhoeffer began *Life Together:* "How very good and pleasant when kindred live together in unity!" (NRSV). She goes on to say:

> The scripture addresses our real hunger as do the words "life together." And yet anyone who has tried to live in community with others knows how beset with pain and difficulties such a life is! Perhaps that is why the pews in our churches are row on row, and why in less obvious ways we have put distance between ourselves and others. We have not wanted to suffer in any serious way the encountering of one another, all unaware that

avoidance deprives us of community that would evoke
in our lives the experience of the psalmist.[10]

Many people in the pews felt the sting of these words not
just in regard to members of their own congregation but
also in regard to the church across the street or down the
block. Moreover, the unity for which O'Connor following
Bonhoeffer strove did not end at the door of the church; the
hunger for community to which they responded was not just
for a community of faith as such, but for something that
gave meaning to the word "community" in a larger context as well. Although the community of the church had
boundaries, disciplines, and characteristics proper to itself,
it was also permeable and carried ramifications for the larger
community. This point is clear in the "four directions" that
emerged from a retreat where the Church of the Saviour
(founded in 1947) was re-visioning its future: "[We dedicate
ourselves] (1) To Christ's church throughout the world; we
are part of the ecumenical church, and want to give ourselves to its life. (2) To the stranger in our midst; we are
called to bring Christ's love to all those whose lives inter-
sect at any point with ours. (3) To the poor and oppressed
of the world. (4) To the building of our common life."[11]

As a result of this report, the congregation formed several
subcongregations, as it were, each with a particular mission
in the larger community. It became a kind of community
ministry turned inside out. Instead of several congregations coming together for mission, one congregation shaped
by mission became, in a sense, several. Like community
ministry, the Church of the Saviour came to emphasize
the point of intersection with the political life of the community. In O'Connor's words: "Community threatens the
established order and in time finds itself in opposition to existing powers. . . . The most basic thing that Jesus does when
he liberates us is to make us caring people who then have
the commission to build communities in the places where
we live and play and work."[12]

This last sentence might have served as a banner for many of the first ecumenical/interfaith community ministries. Both the Church of the Saviour and the East Harlem Protestant Parish, as community ministry precursors, stressed the potential of the congregation as a model of Community (with a capital C) and the strategic significance of the congregation for community building at a time when respect for that institution was at an ebb. We note that they both used covenant terminology to describe the experience of being brought into and given responsibility for a relationship with other believers for the sake of the larger community by virtue of their faith in God.

Repairing the Broken Covenant— The Mission of Community Ministry

The consortiums of local congregations, who busy themselves with issues of the common life of the community, sound the counterpoint to Bellah's despairing title, *The Broken Covenant*.[13] Recently, a coalition of inner-city congregations in upstate New York held an interfaith prayer breakfast to highlight their concern about the negative effect of hostile relations between the city and county governments on all the residents of the area. The meeting resulted in several additional meetings bringing together city and county officials and a listing of those areas where city/county cooperation could be improved. This is an example of how community ministry affirms an embedded interreligious unity and uses it to encourage responsible interactions in the civic sphere.

Where, as in this case, ecumenical/interfaith community ministry gives expression to an embedded unity of believers, it is indebted to the experience, language, and hope of "covenant" in American history. Most see it quintessentially exposited in Massachusetts Bay Colony leader John

Winthrop's sermon aboard the *Arbella*, in which he enjoined his hearers to be true to the covenant into which they "are entered," by being "knit together as one person" in order to follow the counsel of the prophet Micah "to do justly, to love mercy, to walk humbly with their God."[14]

When Rosetta Ross describes African American women "responding to God's faithfulness" (below, p. 24) we come upon this underlying and important theological thread in American intellectual history. This theology is based on the premise that God has taken an initiative to make a covenant with people of faith. God promises to guide, protect, and to be present among the people, and the people respond in faithful gratitude with right actions based on divinely inspired guideposts or laws. A lived covenant theology entails an unshakable trust in a God who is faithful to accompany the people through whatever perils they may have to endure.

Covenant theology almost always has a political cast or referent because the covenant constitutes an entire people with a collective responsibility to God, to each other, and to the wider community. The "Great Commandment," found in both the Hebrew Bible and the New Testament, encapsulates the divine mandate or law for both the religious community and the body politic.

The theology of covenant involves an element of proximateness or small-scale community — an element that Bellah as well as other commentators and historians seem to miss even while describing it. Bellah traces the influence of covenant language, beginning with the agreement made among the American Puritans while still in England and most eloquently articulated for the ages in Winthrop's shipboard sermon, of which we cite a portion here. Note that its immediate context is a community of Christians who have been confined together for several weeks on a ship at sea. The intimacy of the situation lends Winthrop's message a dimension unimaginable if he were writing for readers who were spread throughout a vast landscape. His injunctions assume proximity. His "city set upon a hill" would be

our village or neighborhood. In fact, I would venture that a
theology of covenant almost always involves an element of
proximateness and/or community on a local scale:

> Thus stands the cause between God and us. We are
> entered into Covenant with him for this work.... Now
> the only way to avoid this shipwreck [the breach-
> ing of the covenant] and to provide for our posterity
> is to follow the counsel of Micah, to do justly, to
> love mercy, to walk humbly with our God. For this
> end, we must be knit together in this work as one
> man, we must entertain each other in brotherly affec-
> tion, we must be willing to abridge ourselves of our
> superfluities, for the supply of others' necessities, we
> must uphold a familiar commerce together in all
> meekness, gentleness, patience and liberality, we must
> delight in each other, make others' conditions our own,
> rejoice together, mourn together, labor and suffer to-
> gether, always having before our eyes our commission
> and our community in the work, our community as
> members of the same body... for we must consider
> that we shall be as a city set upon a hill.

We note that Winthrop, a layperson, in paraphrasing the
text from Deuteronomy 30, inserted the words "and to love
one another" — echoing the commandment in Leviticus
(19:18; see also Lev. 19:34 and Deut. 10:19). The two latter
citations are to love the *stranger* as one loves the self and
may be seen as a variation or extension of the commandment to love the neighbor. This insertion is true to the spirit
of the Deuteronomic text itself inasmuch as it is preceded
by "For this commandment, which I command you this day,
is not too hard for you, neither is it far off.... But the word
is very near you; it is in your mouth and in your heart, so
that you can do it." The covenant, the God of the covenant,
the requirements of the covenant, and the opportunities for
fulfilling those requirements are all as close to you as the
nearest person in the community.[15]

In juxtaposing community and covenant, John Winthrop laid down a theological seed-plot that has a peculiar relevance for twenty-first-century community ministry not only because it informs the conversation between the people and institutions shaped by faith and those not necessarily so shaped; not only because it points the way toward a renewing of the social-political fabric in which (in Bellah's terms) new births of freedom move from revolution to constitution and from conversion to covenant; but also because it evokes and invokes a certain local scale that may be more essential for the realization of these hopes than anyone heretofore has estimated.

In *The Broken Covenant*, Bellah makes much of the interreligious dimension because he sees potential therein for an eventual renewal of covenantal civic responsibilities at the local level. In so doing he makes a case for local ecumenical and interfaith community ministry.[16] He opined "common sense utilitarianism [which] has been the dominant mode of American public morality — has torn interest from its larger traditional context and understands it only in terms of the self-interest of the isolated individual."[17] The "broken covenant" refers to the decline and virtual disappearance of the strong note of social responsibility struck in Winthrop's conception of the covenant.

According to Bellah, the covenant is broken also in the sense that many groups — in fact, all groups that are not predominately male, white, Anglo-Saxon Protestants of a certain economic class (with some incremental exceptions in recent history) — have been excluded from the covenant, despite ideals to the contrary. Furthermore, the very mainline faith groups that have supported the traditions of an inclusive covenant no longer have the vitality and intellectual vigor to continue to keep the flames of commitment alive. He despairs, therefore, for the future of America.[18]

Yet I do not. I say that in light of the rise of community ministry and its potential for promulgating the experience, language, and hope of the covenant at the local level, Bellah's despair was at least premature. The embedded unity of congregations in a community, once acknowledged, offers hope that this aspect of the broken covenant — the apparent failure of religious communities to counter the exclusivity and divisions of society — may be repaired.

We might posit with the ethicist Clinton Gardner that there is a broken covenant to be repaired in every age, that, "Viewed in negative terms, the history of mankind [sic] is the story of man's efforts to deny the essential unity of all men in one common humanity."[19] Furthermore, religious communities themselves are very much a part of, perhaps the larger part of this divisive story. Yet, as Gardner as noted, covenant in the biblical and most inclusive sense can never be broken irrevocably because it is initiated and maintained ultimately by the creator and sustainer of the universe. Because covenant, understood in this inclusive way, is applicable to both the faith community and the wider human community, many community ministries have actually drawn up covenants for describing and sealing the relationships among their constituent congregations.

One of Gardner's students, Frederick E. Glennon, would recast the welfare system (with which many community ministries have direct dealings) in terms of covenant.[20] Indeed, the concept does attract those engaged in community ministry who are searching for a theological term, at once both descriptive and normative, with a positive, constructive meaning not only in the religious sphere generally but also in the social-political sphere.[21]

The point here is that a theology that is meaningful to ecumenical/interfaith community ministry stresses accountability both to God and the community. "Community" here refers both to the religious community and to the larger political community of which the religious community is a part. The religious/political term "covenant" rejoins all these triadic relationships. Therefore, congregations of a particular community could do no better than to constitute themselves as intentional, covenanted communities pledged to God and to each other and to the larger local/global community in which they find themselves. The general content of such a pledge (and this might be the only thing that different neighborhoods and localities would have in common) would be that biblical epitome of responsible action: "to love the Holy One, your God, and to love your neighbor as yourself."

Repairing the Broken Covenant (Ia)

Although Bellah drew some encouragement from the growing diversity of religious expression in the United States, he did not acknowledge two theological resources for preserving the covenant themes of civic engagement and responsibility — the mainline predominantly African American denominations and the theology of the laity movement, which represent two potential key supports for any group of congregations who may want to put their embedded unity into action.

Although a few ecumenical/interfaith community ministries have a broad African American involvement and significant African American leadership (the East End Cooperative Ministry of Pittsburgh is a notable example) in the main, community ministry has had great difficulty in making alliances with local predominantly black churches. One of the oldest community ministries in the United States — the Interfaith Community Council of New Albany, Indiana — was founded in 1964 in the wake of the publication of the Kerner Report. A federally mandated commission to study the meaning of the racial riots that were breaking out in cities of the United States issued this report. The commission made the dire prediction of a permanent division of society into two parts — one black and one white. The response of this small city's churches was to try to heal the breach in their own backyard by forming a community ministry that would have this purpose at the top of its agenda. On the first staff, two of the three were African Americans, several African American congregations were in the membership and represented on the board of directors, and the first program to be instituted was to be an integrated recreational and tutorial program for youth. Thirty years later, except for low-paid child-care workers, there were no black staffers; there were no African American congregations in the membership; there were no programs for black or white youth; and the only program that served the black population other than an emergency food pantry was a child-care program that had been served an eviction notice by the predominantly white congregation in which it was housed.

The reasons adduced for this all-too-frequent situation often imply some failing or weakness in the black churches: lack of ecumenical spirit, part-time pastoral leadership, shaky finances, a separatist ideology. But these explanations do not bear scrutiny. Upon closer investigation, one sees a high level of interaction and mutual support among the African American congregations of a typical city, with a correspondingly high level of involvement in community and civic matters. The fact of the matter is that among the so-called mainline churches, local ecumenism is a constant and never-ending task of overcoming historic economic and social barriers as well as lingering racist attitudes and behaviors. On the contrary, among predominantly African American churches, ecumenical relations come as almost second nature — the barriers having long since been overcome in the crucibles of slavery and segregation and in the continuing struggle against systemic racism and classism. In my experience, a vital and living theology supports local ecumenical work in predominantly African American congregations.

At the outset of "A Womanist Model of Responsibility: The Moral Agency of Victoria Way DeLee," Rosetta E. Ross states:

> From the period of slavery in the United States through modern times, black religious women's activism has been guided by a perspective that views duty to God and calling by God as the origin of their work. Sojourner Truth, for example, described herself as called by God to speak against slavery. Around the turn of the century, The National Baptist Women's Convention felt it was their duty to link social generation, racial advancement and spiritual regeneration. After emancipation, many educated black women felt "a strong conviction of duty" to go south to reach newly freed persons.[22]

As a case in point, Ross tells about Victoria Way DeLee, who began volunteer civil rights work as early as 1947. DeLee participated in voter registration campaigns, school desegregation efforts, and an array of other activities, as she tried to improve life for black people in Dorchester County, South Carolina.

It is significant for our purposes to note the very local orientation of DeLee, for my contention is that this level and scale of community formed the matrix of Winthrop's notion of covenant in the first place; and that, to a degree, the covenant might be said to have never been "broken" at this level — especially among African Americans; and that we might look to the very local scene for hope and inspiration for a renewal of political life at the national level. Through community ministry, the interreligious cooperation called for by Bellah, is in fact taking place in the context of the very local. Bellah never quite entertained the possibility that "the deeper sources in our tradition . . . to build a public will for democratic change in America" might be found at this most local level — the level of the urban neighborhood, the suburban area, the small town, or the rural county. If he had looked more closely at the African American and feminist literature and experience as well as the congregational studies literature, it might well have brought him to the point of seriously considering this question of scale.

Equally significant as her local orientation was the inspiration Victoria Way DeLee derived from her African American congregations for her involvement as a teenager in the early civil rights struggle over voting rights and schools in her own neighborhood. The first was the Methodist congregation of her grandmother, then the Baptist church where she met her husband and where she received encouragement to try to register to vote, and finally a Holiness congregation — three distinct traditions but all of them providing inspiration to become engaged responsibly in civic life.

Ross's article contains a compelling story of one woman's ministry clearly based upon a collective and communal understanding of her responsibility for the political life of her community derived from faith in God. "These women act out of their relationship with God, whom they understand as faithful to them, and, therefore, with them in all circumstances." This was no less true in the case of Victoria DeLee, who says she persisted because she saw "God in front leadin' all of us in the work."[23]

One reason that African American churches have preserved, better than others, this covenantal way of speaking of the connections among themselves and with the larger society may be that this way is consonant with African roots. Peter Paris comments:

> The ethical systems of Africans tend to be covenantal.
> That is to say, all relations between persons as well as
> those with the spiritual realm are covenantal in nature.
> In fact, the relationships are reciprocal in that each
> party is bound to the other by bilateral obligations. . . .
> In all their relationships Africans assume reciprocity
> of responsibilities and duties determined, in large part,

by traditional understandings, beliefs, and practices. Such responsibilities and duties were exercised within a context that bestowed primary value on activities of constituting, reconstituting, preserving and enhancing the community.[24]

Words that in the majority white society reinforce individualism may have a different, more communal meaning in an African American church. The word "freedom," for example, may "bolster the value of American individualism" for whites; but for African Americans, a "communal sense of freedom has an internal African rootage curiously reinforced by hostile social convention imposed from outside."[25] The three centuries of slavery and another century of segregation only heightened the sense of collective success or failure and of reliance upon a God who may be relied upon to liberate a faithful people from oppression and injustice.

Victoria DeLee began working on voter registration drives and school desegregation in 1947, years before the passing of the 1964 Civil Rights Act, which, with the *Brown v. Board of Education* decision in 1954, would set in motion the civil rights movement. The "Brown" in *Brown v. Board of Education* was the Rev. Oliver Leon Brown of the St. Mark A.M.E. Church in Topeka, Kansas, who brought suit on behalf of his nine-year-old daughter, Lynda Brown. It was another African American minister — the Rev. Dr. Martin Luther King Jr. — who led the civil rights movement to a moment of triumph in the defeat of segregation in the public transportation system of Montgomery, Alabama, after Rosa Parks and other women brought the issue to a head. It was local black congregations of several denominations acting in concert as a force for justice and responsibility in the civic sphere in town after town that accounted for both the leadership and the rank and file of the civil rights movement.

What may be easily overlooked, however, is that the civil rights movement was also an ecumenical movement —

a *local* ecumenical movement in the African American communities first, and then spreading to touch and eventually embrace large segments of the predominantly white churches, Protestant and Catholic. "Black churches were the major points of mobilization for mass meetings and demonstrations, and black church members fed and housed the civil rights workers from SNCC, CORE, and other religious and secular groups. Most of the local black people, who provided the bodies for the demonstrations, were members of black churches acting out of convictions that were religiously inspired."[26] Local black ecumenism energized the mainline churches,; and many members of those churches experienced an ecumenical conversion through involvement in the civil rights movement. (In a recent round of interviews of veterans of the ecumenical movement in Texas, the author found that for many of these leaders, their involvement in the civil rights movement was decisive in their ecumenical formation.)

Thus, as congregations in any community seek to relate to each other in more responsible ways than heretofore, the African American experience and the churches born from that experience have much to offer them — much to teach them. For one thing,

> The objective of black ecumenism, unlike that of white ecumenical movements, is neither structural unity nor doctrinal consensus; rather, it is the bringing together of the manifold resources of the Black Church to address the circumstances of African-Americans as an oppressed people. It is mission-oriented, emphasizing black development and liberation; it is directed toward securing a position of strength and self-sufficiency.[27]

Black ecumenism addresses life-and-death matters in ways that go beyond help for individuals and extend to social, political, and economic systems. Moreover, black ecumenism tends to seek local solutions for local problems with an emphasis on social change:

[Black] local ecumenical movements arguably face a greater challenge than do most national movements in that they are engaged in a direct and immediate way with the people whose needs they seek to alleviate; they are, in a word, on the front line of the urban battle for the sanctity of human life. Collectively, local ecumenical movements constitute an immensely significant component of the overall story of black ecumenism.[28]

Finally, local black ecumenism has identifiable theological frames of reference that function as touchstones for day-to-day activities. The underlying one and in the background is the covenant. The other, more in the foreground and to some extent an extension or outgrowth of covenant theology, is black liberation theology, about which we speak more in the next chapter. Nowhere do we find both covenant unity and theology more operative than in black church ecumenism — most dramatically in the history of the civil rights movement.

Repairing the Broken Covenant (Part Ib)

The crucial role of African American clergy in the civil rights movement notwithstanding, those years also saw the laity, black and white, come into their own as ministers in their own right — persons who accepted the call not to sit in the back of the bus, not to accept unjust restrictions on voting (see the story of Victoria Way DeLee above). These activists were often "community people" in a way that clergy could never be because of their often itinerant and temporary status. These lay ministers and community people knew for a fact that there were (sometimes literally) brothers and sisters in the faith in the congregations down the street from their own. They were prepared to cooperate, no questions asked. These are the "deeply woven roots" of which Gary Gunderson writes.

At the interpersonal level, the relations among lay members of the various congregations reflect the embedded unity of congregations that we have posited in this chapter. Either as individuals or as representatives of their congregations, they gather and work cooperatively on various community improvement projects — an expression of felt covenantal obligations. Robert Wuthnow's book *Acts of Compassion* is instructive in this respect because it analyzes the motivation of volunteers in faith-related social mission. The results of his research resonate with our particular approach to the theological question.[29]

First, there is the greatest respect for the common life of the immediate community. Seventy-two percent of the volunteers interviewed preferred to work with small, local charities rather than large national ones. Wuthnow characterizes this as a belief "that compassion should have a human face."[30] From our perspective this insight is an indication that the embedded unity that we posited between local congregations does not transfer easily to larger frames of reference.

Second, there is the suggestion that there may be something absolutely essential about the individual's investment in the community if one is to be true to one's best self. Going beyond the call of duty to help others, to fulfill our responsibilities, and to make the society better constitutes caring. Going beyond the call of duty for personal gain, material reward, or mere longings for power and prestige constitutes corruption. The former guards against the latter, or as Elmer Benson put it when asked if there would always be a need for volunteers: "I can't imagine what else people would do," he exclaimed, "except get into trouble."[31] Either one acts as a responsible member of the community or one acts in a manner destructive of the community. This notion, of course, implies the triadic relationship of which we have spoken.

Finally, in the mind of the volunteer there always resides the expectation and hope of the ripple effect, namely, that

"When someone shows compassion to a stranger, it sets in motion a series of relationships that spreads throughout the entire society."[32]

The theology of the laity movement is a reflection of the increasing involvement of Wuthnow's volunteers and the critical roles that they have played in both the ecumenical and social action arenas since the early part of the twentieth century. It was an important factor in preparing the ground for ecumenical and interfaith community ministry.

Richard Broholm is a relatively recent representative of the tradition of the theology of the laity. His ideas were given voice in three essays contained in a volume entitled *The Laity in Ministry*.[33] Prior to Broholm, the theologies of the laity had emphasized the participation of the laity in the traditional church structures and functions, their importance in implementing social change and identifying ethical issues in the "real world," and the theological significance of their vocation in the larger scheme of God's purposes.[34]

Under the influence of the writings of Dietrich Bonhoeffer and his idea of "religionless Christianity," Broholm advocated: (1) "a more decisive way for the church to confirm a secular calling as a valid ministry, and (2) a more meaningful way for laity to experience being conformed to God's will in the exercise of that ministry."[35] Toward these two goals he proposed: (1) public recognition and commissioning of laypersons in the presence of the worshiping community in relation to their ministry at their place of work, and (2) training and organization of laypersons in order to give them the tools to change the institutional structures for the better as they impact both the working environment and the society at large. Broholm took the covenant concept of responsibility for the body politic and applied it not just to political structures as such but to all sorts of collectivities and especially to the institutions where the laity exercised their vocations — hospitals, schools, business corporations, law firms, and so on.

It is to be regretted that today's community ministry only partially if at all reflects the theology of the laity and Broholm's vision. It is well situated, however, to pursue such goals, and there is a persuasive theological mandate to do so.

Chapter 2

The Local Body Politic and Community Ministry

Politics[1]

The daily shootings of youth by youth in the inner cities of America, the shooting of unarmed African Americans by white police officers, the mass shootings by gun-wielding students of their classmates and by former employees of their former colleagues, attacks on government workers, and the threat of international terror all strike fear in the hearts of many. One organization, Interfaith Ministries of Greater Houston, decided to memorialize every one of these violent deaths in their area by an interfaith prayer vigil on the very spot of the occurrence. These vigils were intended to perform multiple functions: They prevented the public at large from becoming inured to the killings; they were a support for the neighborhoods in their attempt to understand and oppose the causes of the shootings; they were a demonstration of respect for the lives of those who were lost; and finally, they brought the faith community together in prayer and supplication on behalf of the larger community. Such vigils, which have been emulated in other parts of the country, demonstrate what is best in community ministry as it is currently practiced. They carry the unitive power of

the faith community into the community at large. In a concrete, imaginative, and meaningful way vigils such as those
in Houston engage the faith communities with a central
issue of the polis or body politic.

In the last chapter, we sought to demonstrate that responsible relationships among congregations are the bedrock of
ecumenical/interfaith community ministry. They are not,
however, ends in themselves. Elizabeth O'Connor said:
"The vocation of Christians is to be builders of communities that join them with what is highest in themselves,
within one another, and within the whole human race."
Thus, the building of community does not end at the boundary of Christianity, nor even at the boundary of the faith
community taken as a whole.[2]

When an interfaith coalition in an upstate New York city
prays for better relations between the city and the surrounding county, it acts *sui generis*. Conversely, when a religious
group promotes or allows hatred of any particular class or
group on the basis of religious belief, it simply and plainly
nullifies itself as a community of faith. Covenant, too, has
been employed perversely to justify divisive and exclusive
aspects of religious faith. Nevertheless, in light of the pre-
ponderance of biblical interpretation, clearly the Hebrew
roots of covenant lend themselves to the more inclusive
reading.

Hebrew Bible theologian Walter Brueggemann says that
covenant language was a part of ancient Israel's internal
conversation "behind the wall" that equipped it for conversation outside of the specifically religious community "on
the wall," as it were. It has, in fact, the same function in
Christianity, and yet it is a public metaphor — derived ultimately not from a source peculiar to itself but rather from
political discourse.[3] "On the wall" is precisely the position of
community ministry — carrying on a conversation with the

wider local community on behalf of the local faith community and the reverse. Thus, the intentional exclusion of, say, a synagogue, on behalf of a "Christian" community ministry, contradicts the mission of the ministry, which may be described as carrying the unitive power of faith into the community at large.

Webber postulated that, studied correctly, scripture would make covenant thinking come alive in the community of the faithful for the benefit of the larger community.[4] Such thinking makes the test of true faith a question of whether it assists in the task of making and keeping us all truly human — not unlike the one described by Peter Paris (above, chapter 1) when he refers to the African heritage of African American churches as "constituting, reconstituting, preserving and advancing the community."

In this respect there is an unmistakable resonance between classical covenant theology and various liberation theologies. They all assume an inherent connection and relationship between politics and theology, ecclesial and societal concerns, the purposes of God and the day-to-day life and governance of any given human settlement. James Cone says that in the black church, every statement of faith is at the same time a political statement.[5] One of Juan Luis Segundo's liberationist principles, for another example, is: "Theology is the Second Step" — the first step being "commitment," which, in turn, is based on realities of the immediate political context.[6]

The Ultimacy of Daily Life and (Therefore) of Local Community

Both politics and theology invest daily life with ultimacy, which is why every community ministry is a theological/ political entity, because it deals at the level of daily life in a specific locality. Whether it relates to a solitary individual (with, say, a problem related to housing), a question of justice involving a whole class of people (for example, discrimination in housing), or a crisis of the entire community (such as an earthquake or flood that destroys dozens of homes), it does so as an expression of a faith in God that is relevant to these and any and all other real-life situations that present themselves.

Community ministry has a potential ally in feminist liberation theology because for it, too, the ultimacy of daily life is axiomatic. The apparent postmodern modesty of this perspective relative to social change disguises an audacious project to reconfigure human community at the most local level possible. Sharon Welch describes it thus:

> The truth of Christian faith is at stake not in terms of its coherence and ontological structures and their potential modification, but in life and death struggles, in daily operations of power/knowledge. The battle against nihilism and oppression is not primarily conceptual but practical. The focus therefore of a liberating faith, ... is ... the creation of redeemed communities.[7]

These sentences may be taken as a rationale for community ministry, but not for just any local cluster of congregations trying to do their social ministry together. Welch sets a certain standard, asking not only for a prior commitment to the poor and oppressed (with Segundo and other Latin American liberation theologians), but asking as well for the courage to minister without the security of "universal truths," which all too often stand in the way of recognizing the particularity of any given community and situation.[8]

Welch's allusion to the "battle against nihilism and oppression" indicates what she has in mind about the ultimacy of daily life — not the romantic idea that ultimacy rests in the mundane, but rather that local, daily life is a battleground between nihilism and oppression on the one hand

and resistance and liberation on the other. What comes immediately to mind are the many literary and historical portrayals of the impact of the rise of National Socialism in Germany and of its insidious pervasion of daily life in locality after locality. As Emil Fackenheim so convincingly teaches, the very character of our own daily life today contains a permanent rupture with the time before the Holocaust. So today our daily life is post-Holocaust life, and the battleground of daily life is all the more fraught with danger of defeat because of it.[9]

Against this backdrop Welch articulates the focus of liberating faith as "the creation of redeemed communities." What is at stake in the struggle to change the character of our daily life is nothing less than the survival of humanity. "Redeemed communities" are not an option. They are a necessity. These are local projects, and truth is in order to each locality.

Regarding the dangers of "universal truths," Gloria Albrecht, following Welch, suggests that truth is always "truth-in-process," in the sense that the search for truth must entail a commitment to empower groups with unequal access to "full participation in the conversation." Herein lies an agenda for community ministry that is made explicit in the following question: "How then can we, as part of the dominant [group or class], begin to form redeemed communities characterized by both justice and nonviolence?"[10]

In response to her question we can do no better than to employ Albrecht's own tripartite approach, using the terms "tradition," "diversity," and "resistance." Her treatment of these reflects the liberationist sensitivity to the importance of local scale, and it resonates with the idea of covenant that links political and theological discourse. The following sections show how an analysis of each of these terms applies directly to the theology and practice of community ministry.

Tradition in Daily Life

A community ministry in the Dallas, Texas, area, which once was a pioneering advocate for the poor, suddenly reversed itself. Among other things, it had developed a model program for educating the poor about benefits, such as food stamps — available to them but not used by a majority of those who were eligible. Upon the hiring of a new executive director, its board laid down an explicit policy of no advocacy — only direct services and only emergency direct services at that. They wanted to be seen as a "pure" charity that did not meddle in the political life of the local community in any way, shape, or form. This kind of decision on the part of a board is not unusual and begs analysis from a theological perspective.

Community ministry arose in the turmoil of the 1960s and spread to a large variety of locations in the United States and abroad in the 1980s. In many cases, individuals who were intent on seeking systemic social change founded these ministries and invoked a new level of cooperation among local religious bodies. Today, one of the ironies of community ministry is that in the vast majority of locations it does not question or challenge the religious and societal traditions with which it must interface on a daily basis.

There are many reasons for this inherent conservatism of the more mature movement: First, being interfaith or ecumenical tends to require a consensus rather than a majority among participating congregations. Second, simply being interfaith and/or ecumenical is sometimes seen and felt as a radical enough departure. Third, many persons would view the delivery of direct services to the poor as the only essential function of community ministry. Fourth, some supporters of community ministry unapologetically tout it as a way to preserve the status quo and to increase the comfort level of the established powers.

For the most part (there are some notable exceptions), community ministry accepts the traditional power arrangements in its community as a given. It seems to have few resources that would allow it to develop a critical perspective on the character of daily life in that community, other than what it might derive from its ecumenical and/or interfaith identity. As such it could become, in fact, a reactionary factor on the local scene with no capacity to uphold divinely mandated (covenantal) responsibilities vis-à-vis the sociopolitical fabric.

In order to avoid a descent into reaction, community ministry might ask itself a series of correlative questions that Albrecht has formulated as we consider the impact of tradition in daily life:

> Agreeing with Hauerwas that we are formed by the practices of our community and the skills we learn there, we must ask how is this acceptable violence rooted in the fleshly existence of this body? [In us and in our daily life and in our practices and habits] What material realities of Christian practices give rise to this "truth"? [This truth that inspires this violence] And what are the material realities that today reproduce these injustices and resist change?[11]

It requires courage to ask these questions, to reflect on their implications for our work, and to act on the implications — to enter on the path of covenantal responsibilities that are entrusted to us.

To be sure, we find resources for this task in study of the Bible; we uncover still more as we critically evaluate the ways in which we have been reading the Bible until now. The task demands that we read the Bible with a healthy suspicion of prevailing mores of biblical exegesis and interpretation.[12] The result may be that a reading of the Bible that subordinates social justice concerns to church growth priorities, that condones an equation between Christianity and a particular culture, that fuels violence against people of another faith, that promotes a business model of congregational life, and that encourages any form of religious hegemony is necessarily challenged.

I believe that there are warrants in our scriptures and traditions for an ecumenical/interfaith engagement with the local community. In fact, I believe that this approach is the one most true to the scriptural plumb lines. The danger is that we minimize our responsibilities in order to be accepted and affirmed in our communities.[13]

Diversity in Daily Life

Generally speaking, community ministry is caught in another contradiction that appears in sharp relief when we view the movement in the light of liberationist and covenantal theologies. It is to the credit of most community ministries that they reflect the variety of people in their community in the makeup of staff and volunteer corps. However, by "diversity" Albrecht does not mean just the presence of a variety of people. She advocates "the empowerment of disqualified knowledge."[14] Although community ministry claims to be in close touch with the needs of the poor by virtue of its direct service contacts, the claim is empty if the ministry does not do its best to "empower disqualified knowledge." Currently, community ministry tends to keep the poor at a distance by emphasizing service to the exclusion of relationship and participation. The diverse knowledge of daily life is denied legitimacy in just the place where one might hope to find it. We would rather, it seems, view the poor as needy than as knowledgeable persons. How can we break through the structures and habits and systems that impact our daily lives to actually see daily life as it is? Can we see through our attempts at charity, which only reinforce our sense of innocence and powerlessness, to uncover the fact that we are not innocent and not powerless, that we are personally implicated in the plight of the poor that come to us, and that we can and ought to do far more than innocently hand out goods and services?[15]

We may experience God through the human diversity of daily life as we recognize and are attentive to the voices from the margins. Albrecht recounts the lessons she learned when she lived for a time among the people of a Catholic parish on the outskirts of San Salvador. There she witnessed violence and death at the hands of a militaristic regime as well as extreme poverty and deprivation. She learned that the "facts" of daily life depend upon your chosen community and its perspective. To express her conviction, Albrecht turned to a metaphor from Rita Nakashima Brock:

> Brock suggests that we image the power of Christ as the power of heart . . . the power of relationship; the power to feel the pains and needs of the oppressed . . . the heart of our capacity to be intimate with our world. . . . This was the gospel we learned from El Salvador — that to be in Christ is to be in the heart of community touching the least of us. . . . To be in Christ is to be one in heart with these others, one in suffering and one in joy, one in life and one in death.[16]

Albrecht challenges us to try to discern the reality behind the reality of our daily lives so that we might know the magnitude of the task of forming redeemed communities. What this means for community ministry is that we evaluate ourselves not just on the basis of material resources that we make available or accessible to people. More important is the quality of relationships that are generated by our efforts as well as the degree to which the marginal members of the community are accorded opportunities for participation and their knowledge is taken into consideration.

Many community ministries form subcorporations for the purpose of instituting programs of community organization, housing, and economic development. Governmental, church, and other private funding for such corporations are often predicated upon the formation of governing boards that include representation of the poor in whose interests activities of these corporations are carried out. For example, the Catholic Campaign for Human Development and the Presbyterian Self-Development of People programs both require that a majority of the boards of the projects they fund be composed of the poor themselves. These are fortuitous requirements that often have nudged community ministries in the direction of the challenge of daily life as understood by Albrecht and other liberationists.

Resistance in Daily Life

In a situation of anticipated increased governmental funding for faith-based organizations, one should not underestimate the importance of interfaith/ecumenical ministry as a sharing of financial resources for the sake of the larger community. Prospective government funding could actually damage intercongregational relations if congregations allowed themselves to be pitted against each other for available public dollars. The fifteen community ministries of the Louisville, Kentucky, metropolitan area have set an example in this regard. They have adopted a cooperative strategy in seeking public, business, and foundation funding, including an open sharing of information relative to funding opportunities and the submission of proposals jointly.

The Louisville coalition is a mild but clear demonstration of "resistance" in daily life because such a noncompetitive posture is not always appreciated in the work-a-day world of philanthropy and community service. One should not imagine that contributors or governments necessarily favor the joint effort of the Louisville community ministries. In spite of all the rhetoric of collaboration that is now in vogue, the rule is that competition is the favored modus operandi;

cooperation is actually suspect. What is meant by "collaboration," as it turns out, is the process by which, in the world of business, mergers eventually develop.

A case in point: A community ministry in southern Indiana applied to a local foundation where the rule was that no applicant receives more than $2,000 per request. The following year, after the foundation had touted the virtues of "collaboration," it initiated a joint grant request with four other community groups for $10,000. Each group would still receive only $2,000, per group but they would be part of a larger cooperative project. The foundation gave the entire project $2,000 — $400 per group! The community ministry and the four other organizations were actually penalized for their cooperation. The lesson here is that resistance in the form of truly cooperative as opposed to competitive models can be costly because it challenges the economic ideology that underlies the status quo. This is the hard reality of even the most timid gestures of resistance in daily life. The illusion of competition must be preserved to mask the reality of privilege.

For an understanding of the system of denominationalism in the United States and its function within a framework of class domination and oppression, H. Richard Niebuhr's classic study, *The Social Sources of Denominationalism* (1929) contains much that is relevant for today. It might be argued that, to the extent that community ministry accepts as given the competitive relationships among its member congregations, it contributes to the perpetuation of class-based social privilege. Unless community ministry is willing to challenge congregations to adopt cooperative rather than competitive modes of relating to one another, it cannot avoid the position of being used as a palliative for problems that require a radically cooperative approach in the quest for just solutions.

If we seriously undertake to learn from the "unqualified knowledges" and if we truly want to counteract the problematic appropriation of our traditions with their built-in social privilege for the dominant groupings to which we belong, then we can hardly not become communities of resistance. But what does resistance mean for those who find themselves in the dominant or oppressive group, as most of the actors in community ministry do? Albrecht suggests the following three steps, which she derives from an article by Marvin Ellison:[17]

The first step is to "decenter" by putting ourselves in those places and situations where we are most likely to hear the voices of those on the margins of society. For example, members of a congregation of which Albrecht was pastor lived for a time in a village in El Salvador where they heard "how the people experienced the behaviors of U.S. corporations and the U.S. government and the myths we tell to sustain the values that justify such behaviors." In that vein, a community ministry could try to establish contact with community-based projects in Latin America or other parts of the developing world. Closer to home, a community ministry might develop forums for itself and for the community where the voices of racial/ethnic minorities, refugees, the disabled, homeless, and other strangers in our midst may be heard.

Next, we are to speak honestly about the power we possess as members of a dominant group, to acknowledge how we came to this dominant position (not entirely by pulling ourselves up by our own bootstraps or by hard work) — "truth telling about ourselves and the ways we defend our privileges."[18] Albrecht asks her class in Business Ethics to write their families' economic histories in order to let the students discover how much gender and race or other privileges contributed to their financial security. She suggests that local churches "reclaim their own institutional histories with an eye to hidden privileges of race and class" and "to look at the way our current practices reflect these privileges and reproduce them."[19]

Finally, we are to hold ourselves accountable for the way we use our privileges and for whose benefit we use them. To recognize that our power as individuals and as parishes is always a relative power, and that there are differences among us as to how much we have, is not to deny the existence of our power. It means that we must identify our specific links to the complex structures that make up our society. We have links to health, financial, and educational institutions, to government, to private industry. Our positions of relative power give us access to other people of relative power, who may listen to people like ourselves in ways they would not listen to others. We are often people who know people who know people.[20] The strength of community ministry lies in this power, and it is magnified by the fact that it can draw on the power of several member congregations and their collective identification with a particular local community. Community ministry is often successful in exploiting these resources to raise funds and to gain acceptance and a measure of prestige in the community. But the question is: to what end does community ministry use the power it possesses? In most cases it probably does not use its power just for self-aggrandizement, but it might more often than not ignore or deny the considerable power it has in order to avoid speaking out on crucial issues and community problems.

Here we have identified some of the reasons that community ministry, although a nontraditional form of social ministry, may tend to be passive rather than critical or prophetic toward received patterns in the local culture. We have attempted to demonstrate also that it is nevertheless incumbent on community ministry to become an authentic community of resistance — one that models the kind of community we seek at large.

Proximity and Awareness

One ministry in the East Liberty section of Pittsburgh opened a shelter for homeless men in facilities made available by one of its member churches — facilities in the church building itself. At the request of the men, a separate

Sunday morning service was organized in those facilities. Although the men ran it themselves with some consultation with clergy of the church, it became an alternative service attended by several from the public at large. For the attendees, the homeless people brought a certain spirit to the service that could not be experienced in another context. When they stood up to pray or to sing or to reflect on the scripture for the day, these were activities that shaped and sustained a community that bridged the gap between the "needy" and their benefactors. The community organization efforts and the personal relationships that developed from the shelter and its worship contributed to making the immediate community and its daily life more human.

Martin Buber's work *I and Thou* influenced all subsequent covenantal and liberationist thought. It is a philosophical/poetic exploration of the "sphere that lies between beings ... the Kingdom that is hidden in our midst."[21] Buber's division of human experience into I-It and I-Thou relationships made it possible for readers to view the commandment to love your neighbor in a new light — to attach a new significance to the proximity implied by the word "neighbor" in the local community and the present moment. Proximity raised the potential of an I-Thou relationship — one that shaped an extraordinary and unique space between, a space where, insofar as every I-It relationship was transcended, Godself might be said to dwell.

For Buber, relationship to the Ultimate always involved a Proximate, and hence always was triadic. Here lies the kernel of the concept of "solidarity," the liberationist term for transcendent human relations, which may be seen as a series of triadic relationships resulting in a "unity of hearts" (Joseph Conrad). Here also we find the root of the concept of decentering in which the I of the I gives way to the Thou of the I — gives way to the capacity for forming the space between — the space of I-Thou where the truth of the relationship holds sway over the universal truths of tradition. This thinking is a welcome obstacle to the objectification of women and men that would classify them as "needy" as opposed to knowledgeable subjects, or that would minimize their suffering at the hands of unjust systems. It is the taproot of any polemic against a rank individualism that is inimical to the right practice of community ministry, as we perceive it.[22]

The "bright building of community" begins with the Proximate — those who hold the promise of "solidarity of relation." Among the Proximate we learn and practice the lessons of responsibility.

In this regard, the ethicist William E. May makes a distinction between what he refers to as "actual" and "constructive" awareness. The former is the immediate perception of a person in a boat with a life preserver who sees someone drowning close by. "Constructive" awareness, on the other hand, is the awareness that ought to arise in those who hold positions of privilege by virtue of those positions.[23]

A part of our privileged status is to have information and also to have the means of responding to it. We have power; we have, in Albrecht's terms, "links to the complex structures that make up our society." Furthermore, in community ministry we have opportunities to deal with the "unqualified knowledges" that define the lack of diversity in our local cultures — placing us all the more in a state of "constructive awareness."

Both liberationists and communitarians elevate the Proximate to revelatory status. Consequently, a unique burden of responsibility rests on ecumenical/interfaith community ministry organizations because of their social location. Proximity confers both an "actual" and a "constructive" awareness of the struggles for survival among the poor and oppressed. Therefore, community ministry must be committed to the poor and oppressed both as poor and oppressed and as humanity, as political and social beings. This is the way of covenant thought, and it requires political engagement.

Local Interfaith/Ecumenical Community Ministry

Interfaith/ecumenical community ministry puts a priority on the local, and a theology of community ministry must take into account its modesty of scale and purview. It must answer to the charges that it suffers from myopia, that it is too enmeshed in the local context to exercise a prophetic role, and that globalization requires regional rather than local structures — that "small" may be neither "beautiful" nor "practical."

"Local" is not a term that, by itself, excludes the global or the regional. Nevertheless, whether one's primary frame of reference is local or global does make a difference theologically. We may go so far as to speak of our community as a "holy mystery," insofar as we assert that God speaks in and through it; and we cannot explain it or fully plumb the depths of it — its secrets of glory as well as of shame, its hidden resources, its incredible potential. The longer our sojourn the more we realize how little we know about it. We do know that when we try to make this community a better place for everyone in it, we grow in faith and in the knowledge of God.[24]

As we have noted, covenant theology tends to assume an element of closeness or limited-scale community. Thus, we make a case for the proposition that this basic metaphor of faith receives its fullest expression, meaning, and efficacy at the most local level possible. The very proximity of the neighbor is what makes the fulfillment of the Great Commandment possible, urgent, and grounded in the daily round. In the Parable of the Good Samaritan the neighbor is not the receiver so much as the giver of life. The parable ensues upon a lawyer's question: "And who is my neighbor?" The neighbor was not of the questioner's faith but was, nevertheless, fulfilling the law and the covenant by his actions toward the half-dead man. Jesus was not asking the lawyer to understand what constituted neighborly actions (There would have been no need of a Samaritan in the story to show that). Rather he was showing that a person — a neighbor, who did not believe or practice the lawyer's religion, could accomplish these deeds, which constituted a fulfilling of the law. The lawyer, the Samaritan, and the victim of crime — all the characters in the parable — were or could have been part of the same local community. The point is clear because these characters peopled the lawyer's daily life.

What the Good Samaritan did is what Welch calls a "contemporary action," which means the shaping of "a matrix in which further actions are possible, the creation of the conditions of possibility for desired changes."[25] This matrix of possibility is, above all, a local phenomenon. This is the essence of the best in the American tradition of religio-political covenanting from John Winthrop until today — the creation of a local matrix of possibility.

Repairing the Broken Covenant (II)

If local community is potentially a "matrix of possibility," then congregations and their community ministry organizations must set the tone. In community ministry, however, imperfect covenants frequently reveal themselves. In one instance, a community ministry board, representing its member congregations, came to the conclusion that the community had a pressing need for affordable child care. It placed a priority on expanding its child-care programs, including building new facilities and using more space in its member churches. Just as the ministry was completing its expansion, one large denomination began to tout the advantages of congregation-based childcare programs as a

way of helping to stabilize local church finances. Several
of the ministry's member churches, which were of that denomination, thereupon decided to start their own child-care
programs. Because the child-care programs in the separate
churches could not subsidize indigent families' child-care
needs to the extent that the interfaith state-certified program could, they, in effect, served only the families that
could afford to pay the market rate — the families from
whom they stood to gain financially. This drain on the
enrollment had the effect of "ghettoizing" the interfaith program as its enrollment went from approximately 40 percent
subsidized children to 95 percent. The churches let their
(now) underfunded interfaith program cover the children
from the other side of the tracks while they took care of
their own children in superior facilities. Eventually, not only
the child-care program but other programs as well had to be
either curtailed or closed.

Variations of the above scenario have been played out across
the country in the recent past. It is true that state and federal policy may have been more deleterious to the provision
of affordable, quality child care in our communities than
the unilateral actions of individual congregations (see p. 83
below). Yet the actions of one denomination's congregations
in this case, in addition to harming the fabric of child-care
services, negatively affected intercongregational relations
and relations between the community ministry and the
wider community. My point is that the basic problem here
was theological: the community ministry had not constituted itself on a firm enough foundation. If it had, it had
allowed the foundation to become weak with the passing of
the years and the changing of congregational leadership, or
the offending congregations simply chose not to respect the
theological foundations of their relationships. How important it is to begin with and maintain sound relationships

between participating congregations, with theological foundations that serve the depth of cooperation they hope to promote in the wider community!

Should it not be self-evident that people of faith can hardly expect to tear down the hostile and dividing walls in the community without first addressing the divisions among themselves? Through the careful formation of an interfaith/ecumenical community ministry, clusters of congregations may address their divisions and thus position themselves for effective joint social missions. I say "careful" because this is a matter of congregations holding each other accountable to share resources and to accept responsibility for maintaining cooperative relationships for the sake of the larger community.

As far as I can tell, the term "beloved community" was introduced by Josiah Royce.[26] He did not use the term in the way that Martin Luther King Jr. did, or as we appropriate it here in the heading of our final chapter. In these instances, the term refers to a potential quality of the body politic. But for Royce, the term applied to the church, which he saw as the precursor and model for the coming "universal community" of all humankind. He took the position that the value of communities surpasses that of the values and interests of individuals.[27] In the church we experience a certain kinship, making it both a "beloved community" and an exemplary one.

Royce's insight was that the primary means by which congregations jointly contribute to the building of redeemed communities is by example — an echo of John Winthrop appealing to the little band on the *Arbella* to relate to each other as a covenanted people. They were to be a "city set upon a hill" — an illustration of the hope that "the community may be to the individual both beautiful and sublime."[28] Ministry by example by no means excludes the many other strategies that are available to an organization. But the first means of impact — first in time, first in effectiveness, and first in theological priorities — is the example we set in our interreligious relations. Theologically, this is without question where to begin. To become a redeemed community, to be formed as a matrix of possibility, to practice love of God and neighbor among us, to enter ourselves into the space of I-Thou, these are the first motions of authentic social mission.

Chapter 3

Community Ministry in
Theological/Historical Context—
An Excursion

Introduction
Community Ministry: An Unpredictable Factor
on the Interfaith and Ecumenical
Relations Scene

In this chapter we temporarily suspend our local focus and for a time hover, as it were, just above the ground in the more general realm of theologies and institutions that effect ecumenical and interfaith relations at the local level. Two considerations enter into this reflection. First, congregations respond to expressions of their particular faith communities that transcend their locales. A Methodist congregation, for example, responds daily to "Methodism" as an authority, as a national and global administration, as a system of belief, as a historical backdrop, as a reference frame and resource for most of its activities, and as an ecclesiastical culture. Yet "Methodism" cannot know the same concrete unity with other faith communities that its local congregations experience.

Denominations, moreover, may not always encourage their congregations to acknowledge a prior unity. Their congregations might experience some tension as they try to respond to both the smaller (ecumenical/interfaith in situ) and the larger (denominational) contexts. It is therefore necessary and desirable to understand the theological warrants for the claim of a neighborhood on the resources of its congregations. Denominations are almost never likely to question a congregation for a "go it alone" stance vis-à-vis its neighborhood, and for good reason! The congregations are the conduits for the financial lifeblood of the denomination. So it is precisely at the local level that denominations have the most difficulty in making good on their ecumenical and interfaith commitments. This is why community ministry might be considered a "wild card" — unpredictable in its impact on established religious systems.[1]

We must also take into account the trans-local cultural differences that might present obstacles to joint community ministry. Surely the most glaring example of unattended cultural disjunction is between predominantly European American and African American congregations. There are other cultural disparities that tend to divide people of faith in the locality for which they are given joint responsibility. Hispanic American, Asian American, Native American, Muslim, Hindu, and Buddhist cultures all present a challenge to find a theological space into which they might enter with equal degrees of comfort or discomfort as the case may be.[2]

Trans-local faith communities and cultures present certain issues for formulating theological underpinnings of interfaith/ecumenical community ministry, which I shall address in two parts: First, the "Quest for a Theology of Local Interfaith and Ecumenical Relations," and second, "Starting Points for a Theology of Local Interfaith and Ecumenical Relations."

The Quest for a Theology of Local Interfaith and Ecumenical Relations

Lack of Consensus

Content to cooperate up to a point, some congregations feel more secure in their participation in community ministry when there is no implied consensus on theological issues. One Missouri Synod Lutheran pastor, who supported his congregation's participation in community ministry, made the above point to the author in so many words. His position is itself a theological one, of course. It holds that each congregation participates on the basis of its own theology. If there were a theological consensus, so he might reason, the congregations would unite, and there would be no need for a coalition of separate religious entities.

The way of least resistance is not to question this pastor's point of view. The participation of the congregation is thus assured, but at a high price. First, it devalues the relationship among congregations — the embedded unity of which we spoke in chapter 1. Second, it practically assures that the operations of the ministry are restricted to the delivery of direct services, because other more systemic and less individualistic social mission strategies may well require a common theological compass. What is needed, then, is a usable theology of interfaith and ecumenical relations, notwithstanding the fact that such a quest might endanger the "easy" participation of a congregation such as the one cited above. This is a search that does not deny the distinctness of the theologies of participating congregations; but at the same time it insists on trying to articulate the meaning of their relationship in common theological terms.

In many ways, an earlier ecumenical movement anticipated this quest and provided initial impetus for it — precisely in theological terms. Such was the case in regard to

the theology of the laity (see pp. 27–30 above). Yet the earlier movement embraced a christocentric theology that was
not applicable beyond the boundaries of Christianity. It was
not the intention of the founders of the World Council or
National Council of Churches to erect such barriers, to be
sure. They thought they could relate perfectly well to other
faiths using a christocentric model. But the result was that
Christianity related to the other faiths mainly as a competitor. In contrast with the older ecumenical movement,
whose beginnings spanned the first half of the twentieth
century, culminating in a glorious moment of antifascist
resistance in Europe, community ministry is congregation-
based, embraces a wider spectrum of denominations and
faiths, is overseen by local lay boards for the most part, and
is eclectic in terms of from where it draws leadership and
intellectual strength — all factors that do not necessarily
encourage theological reflection.[3]

In the 1960s community ministries began to spring up
throughout Canada and the United States in spontaneous
fashion. The stress on social ministry "at the most local
level possible" set this movement apart from the earlier ecumenism. In 1985, I formulated a definition of community
ministry that seems to have held up over the years:

> Community Ministry is a variety of services (min-
> istries), activities, advocacy, projects, and programs
> which are performed as a social mission by the mem-
> bership of and on behalf of several congregations of
> different denominations or faiths within certain ge-
> ographical limits which are jointly defined by the
> congregations as the boundaries of their local commu-
> nity or area of service.[4]

In retrospect, it is striking that, as descriptive as this definition may be, it contains no theology as such. In fact, this
definition is painfully accurate insofar as there has been pre-
cious little reflection, let alone consensus, on the meaning
of this locally focused interfaith/ecumenical ministry.

Kenotic Theology

Kenotic theology — an ecumenical theology that was a development on the christocentric theology of the earlier ecumenical movement — served as a midwife to a period of extensive experimentation out of which came, among other phenomena, community ministry.[5] This theology, represented popularly by Colin Williams's books, also produced an actual structural vision for community ministry in the writings of Steve Rose.[6]

Williams's books were a reporting out of the National Council of Churches' study process: "The Missionary Structure of the Congregation." They emphasized "humanity coming of age" and the signs of God's work in an increasingly secular world. The churches should take their cue from such signs as they engage the changing structures of the world where God is moving in the *avant garde.*

A basic assumption of these works was that the local parish was becoming an anachronism, and that the church might take more appropriate local forms as it responds to the accelerating rate of social change.[7] Steve Rose wanted cooperative, ecumenical ministries that would serve as a vehicle for a massive transfer of assets from the congregations to other forms of local ministry. This, in fact, happened to some degree in some areas, and nascent community ministries benefited from it.[8]

From the standpoint of community ministry, however, the kenotic theology had three major flaws: First, local congregations were the building blocks of community ministry. Its practitioners saw, in advance of the congregational studies movement, that congregations, far from being anachronistic, were vital subcultures with their own languages, myths, and identities that, when brought together, produced a synergism that was valuable for the community. Second, congregations were the source of people, facilities, and funds from which all other programs and projects flowed. Without a congregational base, there would be abandonment of neighborhoods — no community organization, housing, and economic development projects, or other community building endeavors. So, although this theology helped give rise to the community ministry movement because of its deconstructive elements, it could not nourish or maintain the movement theologically. It failed to supply an intrinsically positive statement about the congregation as an ecumenical institution.[9]

Finally, kenotic theology emanated from a narrow, white, Protestant spectrum just as community ministry was becoming in almost every instance a Catholic/Protestant mix, including in many instances predominantly African American congregations and also some synagogues. This theology hardly resonated at all with the wider spectrum — not only because of its christological orientation but also because "abandonment" was seen as a threat to the unique identity and contribution of various groups. Ironically, "abandonment" might have resulted in a kind of white Protestant hegemony over cooperative efforts!

Liberation Theology

About the time that kenotic theology was revealing its weaknesses in regard to interfaith relations and local social mission, liberation theology burst upon the scene with the publication in English of *A Theology of Liberation* by Gustavo Gutiérrez in 1973.[10]

Written originally in Spanish by a Roman Catholic speaking out of a Latin American context, it gained an immediate hearing in North America. Its effect was both to encourage and to critique the nascent community ministry movement.

Two liberation theology words already very much in vogue among people engaged in social ministry in the 1960s were "alienation" and "renewal." "Alienation" referred to a felt sense of fragmentation and division in American society. A proposal for a community ministry at the time begins with the following paragraph:

We note that there are many signs of alienation or brokenness in the society in which we live. We are separated on the basis of age, color, and place of residence, job or income classification. All of us suffer from these various forms of separation insofar as they contribute to our inner loneliness and lack of harmony.[11]

Borrowing from Marxist literature, liberation theology offered a concrete interpretation of the meaning of alienation in terms of economic injustice. Psychoanalytical thought and existentialist philosophy also informed the word. Thus, "alienation" signified a broad-based negative commentary on modern post–World War II life.

The word "renewal" reflected a powerful counteremotion of the period. There was a sense that just around the bend there was a new age waiting to be born. The community ministry proposal cited above put it in these terms:

We affirm, nevertheless, that a spirit of renewal is present and at work in our society. We declare that it is this spirit of renewal that has brought us together from many varied backgrounds and traditions. . . . In general, our common confidence in the spirit of renewal causes us to hope for a new day and a new life for our society and leads us to find ways of celebrating its coming. We invite all people from all segments of society to join in this celebration and in this ministry of renewal. . . .

In spite of the assassinations of Martin Luther King Jr. and Sen. Robert Kennedy, the ongoing undeclared Vietnam War, and the mounting evidence that the demon of racism had not yet been conquered, people of goodwill were coming together to reassert the power for renewal captured in Mary's prayer:

My soul magnifies the Holy One, for You have regarded the low estate of your handmaiden. . . . You have scattered the proud in the imagination of their hearts, You have put down the mighty from their thrones, and exalted those of low degree. You have filled the hungry with good things and the rich You have sent empty away. (Luke 1:46–55)

Gutiérrez says of this prayer, which is central to his theology: "The future of history belongs to the poor and exploited. True liberation will be the work of the oppressed themselves; in them the Lord saves history."[12]

Liberation theology is an ecumenical theology that speaks uniquely to the community ministry scene. Community ministry and liberation theology are contemporaries. Each entered the world about the time of the Second Vatican Council, and their initial period of development ran to the beginning of the nineties — from the disillusioned end of the post–World War II period to the collapse of Eastern bloc communism and the discrediting of Marxism as a political/economic ideology. Whereas liberation theology was a clarion call to hear God's preferential option for the poor of the South, community ministry might be viewed as an attempt to salvage an authentic response to Mary's prayer in the North by focusing on the purely local.

Liberation theology may be seen as an astute interpretation of what the Great Commandment means specifically for our own time. In a key passage Gutiérrez describes the same triadic relationship that we heard in the sermon of John Winthrop aboard the *Arbella*.[13] The faithful discharge their obligation to God in their relationship to the neighbor. Where there is justice and righteousness toward the neighbor there is also knowledge and love of God. Gutiérrez's special relevance for us lies in his persistence in defining these relationships in terms of economic justice — grounding his argument in both the scriptures and in his own immediate context, one that becomes our own in view of the economic interdependence of North and South.

With its emphasis on economic justice for the neighbor, Latin American liberation theology affirmed the local orientation of community ministry while mitigating its myopia. It opened community ministry to the influence of the "ecclesial base communities." These communities of worship, Bible study, and action offered an alternative, locally focused life. They afforded a model for effective, faith-based resistance to an oppressive political system — a "community of solidarity and resistance," to use Welch's phrase. Moreover, like community ministry at its start, only more so, the base community was a reaction to the inaction of denominational and ecumenical officialdom in the face of oppressive political and economic developments at the national level.[14]

Richard Shaull's call for a North American equivalent of the base community was implicitly ecumenical. In fact he compared the base community movement to the sixteenth-century Radical Reformation, saying that a Protestant could better understand liberation theology if he or she studied the Anabaptist wing of the Reformation.[15] Shaull and others made it clear that the base communities were a potential model for North American Protestants as well as for Latin American Catholics. They, in effect, lent a kind of Protestant imprimatur to Gutiérrez's initiative.

If Bonhoeffer and then Webber and O'Connor opened new perspectives on religious community without kicking over the traces (chapter 1), and if later liberation theologies and biblical studies provided a new way of viewing the civil community and civic responsibility (chapter 2), then Gutiérrez and his interlocutors cleared a new path to ecumenical theology amidst a plethora of ecclesiastical and theological experimentation — one that upheld the oppressed, the poor and the weak as instruments of God's favor and revelation for every believer of every faith.

A Theology of Liberation created a stir among those involved in the kenotic experiments of the time because of its attempt to reclaim the tradition rather than throw it out.

Those who were looking for a different kind of congregation (see above p. 14) responded favorably to the notion of a North American equivalent to the base community. In some Catholic parishes, small groups began to meet regularly in private homes for a celebration of the Mass, Bible study, and reflection on the social aspects of their lives. Against their canons, Catholics invited their Protestant neighbors to participate fully in these services. Some Catholic laity became involved in community ministry out of a desire to find a North American equivalent to the base community. Among Protestants, new impetus was given to the house church movement. Some community ministries tried at the same time to become worshiping communities — some on an ecumenical basis. Community ministries found that many of their volunteers counted their participation as an alternative to involvement in a traditional congregation or parish.

Just as community ministry in the North tended to replace moribund local councils of churches and introduced a new model of ecumenical relations at the local level, the Latin American base community replaced the parish as the most local level of ecclesial participation and the point of intersection between the church and primary societal institutions. Just as community ministry opened up a new avenue for lay ministry and converted local ecumenism to a movement that was primarily lay driven, the base community opened almost every function of ministry to the laity.

But these parallels notwithstanding, community ministry never became a North American equivalent to the base community movement, and although the base communities inspired a theology, community ministry did not.[16] Community ministry tended to fend off theologies — both the christocentric theology of the older ecumenical movement and, later, the kenotic theology with its anticongregational bias. Ultimately, liberation theology, too, although it could

be adduced to support ecumenical and interfaith community ministry, proved problematic for the practitioners of
community ministry. It was antipathetic to community
ministry where the latter uncritically took on the color of
American culture. (The truth is that these ministries were
and are ultrasensitive to local mores. In many places, just
one act of advocacy on behalf of gay/lesbian liberation, for
example, would almost certainly result in the closing of their
doors.)

Public enemy No. 1 for classical liberation theology is the
transnational corporation (TNC). But we need only look
around us to appreciate the extent to which TNCs per-
vade every aspect of local community life. Chances are, the
largest provider of jobs in the community is a TNC. Much
of the fund-raising on behalf of community ministry is directed toward TNCs or their corporate personnel and other
extensions such as the banks of the community. When it
comes to recruiting ecumenically minded, faith-motivated,
ethically sensitive, and socially progressive individuals for
community ministry boards, some of these recruits will be
employees — "agents," if you will — of TNCs. Furthermore
the finances of the local congregations that compose the
backbone of community ministry are inextricably entangled
with TNCs. If we are honest about it we will not deny that
the TNC is as omnipresent in community ministry as the
very air we breathe.[17]

Our task, therefore, is to find an authentic theology that
can live and function for us "in the belly of the whale."
Sharon Welch, with her emphasis on the local, would probably urge that we not give up on the liberationist agenda.[18]
But community ministry is not well positioned to follow
a dualistic *modus operandi*. Whether or not liberation theology can be accused of classical dualism, its application
seems to imply a dualistic cosmology: the forces of the poor
that carry the valence of revelation versus the TNCs, which
are instruments of economic and political oppression — the
epitomes of institutional violence.

The reality is that, for all of the resonance between liberation theology and community ministry, in almost every community just the attempt to bring together people of different religious persuasions for the purpose of cooperative action may be taken as a challenge to accepted cultural, political, and economic arrangements in that very community. The embedded unity of which we speak is not necessarily supported by these arrangements. So from the very start a community ministry is vulnerable and may easily fall into a timid and apologetic style. It requires a theology that both articulates the embedded unity and affirms and expands its capacity to act forthrightly. Certainly community ministry itself needs to be liberated.

The Liberation of Community Ministry

A theology appropriate to community ministry blesses interfaith and ecumenical cooperation, frees it from yearning toward the centers of power where it and its member congregations would compete for the prizes of prestige and control, without cutting it adrift from the local community.

For Walter Wink, the problem is the *system* of oppression that plagues human life. According to Wink, Jesus' mission was to oppose this system and to save humanity from it. Wink, with the liberation theologians, identifies neoliberal capitalism as indicative of the values of the domination system for today:

> Profit is the highest good. Consumerism has become the only universally available mode of participation in modern society. The work ethic has been replaced by the consumption ethic, the cathedral by the skyscraper. The Kingdom of Mammon exercises constraint by invisible claims and drives its slaves by invisible prods ... but Mammon is wiser in its way than the dictator, for money enslaves not by force but by love.[19]

Wink's concept of the domination system supplements liberation theology in two important ways for the purposes of community ministry. First, he does not seek to localize the forces of evil in any one institution over others (e.g., the transnational corporation) or set of institutions (e.g., economic ones) but recognizes that the oppressive forces permeate all aspects of our existence. What we have to deal with is a systemic phenomenon that reaches into the churches themselves and their scriptures and which predates them. One does not get to the roots of the problem by demonizing the transnational corporation. The domination system *endures* from generation to generation. The awareness that our lives are inescapably interwoven with transnational corporations is only a stage leading to recognition that the very structures of our existence are infected by the domination system. The hallmark of this system is the violence perpetrated at every level, direct and indirect, personal and collective, overt and systemic or covert, against humanity but also against the earth and other forms of life.[20]

The violence that our local communities experience "unmasks" (to use Wink's term) the domination system for what it is — real, pervasive, and violent. I contend that local religious communities constitute a countervailing force by the quality of the relationships among themselves if their eyes and ears are opened to the local effects of the domination system past and present on the entire community. Community ministry may thus model an alternative system for the community.[21]

Another aspect of Wink's thought which has relevance for community ministry is the affirmation that the myth of redemptive violence (see p. 127, note 20) is not a true portrayal of our origins or destination. We are not prisoners to this violent identity; "the powers," though fallen, are good in origin and will be, are being, redeemed. According to Wink, a Christian cosmology does not allow for a demonization of the powers as such. The powers are redeemable. They are not in themselves evil, but they may be the diseased purveyors of evil. In his exposition of Colossians 1:16–17 Wink writes:

> The Principalities and Powers that visit the world with so much evil are not autonomous, not independent, not eternal, not utterly depraved. The social structures of reality are creations of God. . . . These powers are the necessary social structures of human life, and it is not a matter of indifference to God that they exist. God made them. . . . Like a cancer, again, they are able to do evil only by means of processes imbedded in them as a result of their good creation.[22]

For community ministry to be effective it must have vital and meaningful interaction with local institutions — the school, city hall, bank, hospital, social service and other religion-based networks, both the nonprofit and business worlds. To do so it must be able to view this infrastructure in some other way than just to see its obvious co-optation by the domination system. Liberation theology tends to view this entire scene of local institutions only in light of their collusion with the oppressive economic system. They belong, individually and collectively, to the class of oppressors. The truth of this view often is all too obvious. But in order to be able to act constructively, in order for community ministry to be enough part of the community to be part of the solution, it must be able to regard this complex of local institutions as redeemable.

They/we are the oppressors, yes; but they/we have the potential to be something else. They/we are redeemable. Thus Wink: "The simultaneity of creation, fall and redemption means that God at one and same time upholds a given political or economic system, condemns that system insofar as it is destructive of full human actualization, and presses for its transformation into a more humane order."[23] This holds for ecclesiastical and faith systems as well as for political and economic ones.[24]

Liberation theology posited a covenant with the poor and oppressed of Latin America for the ultimate well-being of both the oppressed and the oppressor. Community ministry, on the other hand, must rely upon a covenant, not yet abrogated, with the oppressors — calling them/us back to their/our true identity, back to the commandment to love God and the neighbor, calling them/us back to a position of reconciliation and solidarity with precisely those whom they/we have oppressed. Such a theology would liberate community ministry from the conditions that now constrain it: old, exclusive religious arrangements and stagnant, unjust ecumenical structures, cultural isolation and increasing collusion with oppressive systems. It would build on the embedded unities that underlie the current competitive configurations of faith, toward cooperation and participation in local community, cooperation and mutual respect among religions, and cooperation and conservation on behalf of Earth, our home.

Starting Points for a Theology of Local Interfaith and Ecumenical Relations

The Nature of the Unity We Seek

There is a discernible pattern in the beginnings of various community ministries. The realization of unity among congregations was preceded by the need for greater unity in the community at large: A tornado, a crisis in racial relations, a chaotic and fragmented new suburb — all led to productive and enduring relationships among local congregations.

Just as the World Council of Churches was indebted in its founding to the collaboration of churches in resistance to fascism during World War II, and just as many ecumenical configurations in the United States owe their beginnings to the civil rights movement, community ministry owes it origins to a spirit of renewal and unity that appeared simultaneously in several local communities.

History proves an inescapable theological reality: unity and harmony among people of different religious beliefs is predicated upon the priority of the unity of humankind. Christian unity is not an end in itself (which is made abundantly clear already in the key text, the high priestly prayer of Jesus in the seventeenth chapter of the Gospel of John); nor is interreligious unity an end in itself (the bloody history of interreligious slaughter attests to the futility of it).

This question of the relative priority of efforts toward unity is as crucial for local communities as it is in the worldwide missiological debates. We take our stand at the local level with those who, at the worldwide level, argue the cause of humanity and Earth. One of those is Philip Potter, who cites approvingly the report of the Faith and Order Commission of the World Council of Churches at Bristol, England, in 1967: "Unity means reconciliation, and the object of God's reconciling work is the created world. . . . What is the function of the Church in relation to the unifying purpose of God for the world? What, then, is the relation of the churches' quest for unity among themselves to the hope for unity among mankind [*sic*]?"[25] Potter made his comments at a time of serious backlash against the Programme to Combat Racism that was mandated by the WCC Assembly in Uppsala in 1968. Potter clearly is arguing for a priority of healing divisions that affect all of humanity, of which racism may be the chief offender. But another major divisive force is religion itself, so that work in this field, too, for Potter, reflects the priority on the unity of humankind.

Potter's words and their relevance to antiracism efforts are particularly applicable to community ministry; they challenge community ministry to consider the unfinished antiracism agenda in almost every American community. We speak of a division in the social fabric both pronounced and seemingly intractable. Its subtle visibility puts community ministry into the ethical position of "constructive awareness" (May, p. 45 above), making it unconscionable not to be combating racism concretely in every locality on an ecumenical and interfaith basis.

I want to emphasize, however, that in the struggles to end or transform the divisions in humanity, it is not a chronology of "first, the church; then, interfaith relations; and finally humanity," which might allow us to sidestep or delay our participation in these struggles. Rather, *the realization of the unity of believers is predicated upon working together on the overarching goal of greater unity among humanity in each local community.* This is the one, great, and brute theological fact that confronts every ecumenical and interfaith endeavor, conference, or ceremony.

It is, of course, possible (perhaps inevitable) that a superordinate agenda of harmony among humankind might actually aggravate historical differences among Christians even while it opens new vistas of unity among them. Karen Armstrong describes how every generation and every religion (specifically, Christianity, Islam, and Judaism) are susceptible to this phenomenon, which results in a realignment of parties within that religion.[26] A religious organization that attempts to relate to the larger agenda of the unity of humanity will likely experience an atavistic reaction by those who fear "impure" elements intruding on their faith or who fear the loss of power and control of the organization's course. We have noted elsewhere how vulnerable community ministry is to these powerful emotions.

Thus, in the divisions of Christianity and in the lack of cooperation between faiths, we have symptoms of a diseased larger system that produces a divided and warring humanity. Therefore, it is futile to make Christian unity a goal in itself insofar as any emphasis on unity that embraces less than the unity of humankind contains an inner tendency to become increasingly more exclusive. In the local community, Christian unity as a goal in itself may quickly become the unity of a particular congregation or a particular denomination in competition with other congregations or denominations.

The Inherent Radicality of Authentic Interfaith and Ecumenical Relations

When an Episcopal priest looked back upon almost forty years of ecumenical and interfaith involvement in Houston, Texas, his comment was, "We didn't have to be radical to be radical."[27] What he meant was that the Texas ecumenists from the 1950s onward did not take stands with the knowledge that they would be seen as radical. They did, however, try to be faithful to each other in their relationships and accountable to each other in terms of their joint impact on the larger community. This double, covenantal commitment led them inevitably to positions that challenged the accepted cultural biases of their local communities. For one thing, it led them, more than their counterparts in other states, into the front lines of the civil rights movement, including early social action ministries on the border and, in Houston, one of the earliest protests against police brutality. There they also formed an impressive network of community ministry, which included organizations in almost every neighborhood of the city.[28]

As time went on, the ecumenists of Texas discovered themselves as a countercultural force in regard to issues that affected the character of local community, but this self-discovery came with an element of surprise. Such was not their intention.

We may witness similar self-discoveries today in the context of local ecological crises. Where people of faith gather to protect their communities, they may find themselves engaged in root-and-branch critiques of systems that endanger both their local and global earthly home. Authentic interfaith and ecumenical relations have this unpredictable character and, as we have noted, just bringing together people of different faiths and denominations may, in some communities, be seen as a threat to the status quo.

One of the best indications that a ministry is ready to "own" its potential for independence from the local culture is its willingness to transition from an ecumenical to an interreligious identity. In a conversation with several executive directors of Louisville community ministries, if there was any one single factor that demonstrated openness to crossing the threshold to deeper relationships between congregations and a more complete response to the community, it was the decision to become an interreligious entity.[29]

Religions, more than denominations, represent a variety of distinct ethnic and national cultures. Therefore just to commit to the local expression of another religion may effectively bring congregations into a social mission that goes beyond direct services. A statement of the National Council of Churches acknowledges this factor. It calls for a recommitment to the pursuit of "religious liberty and religious freedom for all" and for a defense of "the rights and liberties of cultural, racial and religious minorities." The statement also recommends "to condemn all forms of religious, ethnic, and racial bias, especially anti-Semitic, anti-Muslim, anti-Asian, and anti-Native American bias, ... and commit the Council and our churches to uproot all that might contribute to such prejudice in our teaching life, and ministries."[30] Interfaith relationships on the local level, therefore, may actually require a certain independence from the majority culture if they are to be affirmed and maintained with integrity.

It would appear, then, that the most effective and logical avenue available to a community ministry that wants to "decenter" itself would be to deepen and broaden the relationships that lie at the heart of the ecumenical/interfaith organization. It is the author's contention that such a course inevitably leads to deeper levels of radicality and responsibility vis-à-vis the surrounding culture.[31]

It is in the interests of the "domination system" (Wink; see above, p. 62) that the religions of the world war against each other and that the Christian denominations compete instead of cooperating. H. Richard Niebuhr made the case that the denominational system is a product of certain American economic interests. On any given day we may witness how tyrants exploit religious divisions for their own purposes. In certain countries the very words "ecumenical" and "interfaith" along with "multicultural" are regarded as subversive. As we have already noted, in the 1964 right-wing coup in Brazil, the Catholic and Protestant conservative wings assisted the perpetrators of the coup in an attempt to root out the ecumenical movement in Brazil.

When the words "interfaith" and "ecumenical" are not regarded as subversive by the established powers, therefore, there may be something amiss; the relationships and ideals carried by these words, when they are implemented, oppose any notion, idea, or system of domination. If, with Wink, we interpret Jesus as one who resisted the relations of domination and subjugation and who opposed a hankering after power and wealth in favor of mutuality in service, then what Jesus did and said might serve as an antidote to the tendency of congregations in any local community ministry to halt the decentering process set in motion by their commitment to each other. Mutual regard, respect, and cooperation need to be constantly rejuvenated lest past visions of prestigious connections to power regain the upper hand.

By way of illustrating the above point, the "welfare to work" agenda in the United States distracts us from our real agenda by the flattering suggestion that faith-based programs can and should supplant government programs to assist the poor and needy.

Significantly enough, nowhere in the various proposals to shift this responsibility to religious organizations is there any mention that ecumenical and interfaith clusters as opposed to isolated congregations competing with each other might better perform the function. Their view of the religious community was strictly utilitarian — that it should be at the service of a laissez-faire economic ethos. A door has been opened to the inner circles of power relative to welfare reform; it is a trap door that would neutralize and compromise the identity of community ministry as an ecumenical and interfaith endeavor — placing it in competitive relationships with other religious entities seeking a "market share" in the business of serving the poor.

The theological significance of government as envisioned by Winthrop and the Puritans was that it performed the diaconal function for the society as a whole. It was the responsibility of government to promote the "general welfare" and to express the God-given mandate to lift up the lowliest and to establish equity/justice for the protection of the weak against the strong. In the covenant there was a unity of purpose embracing the state, the church, the citizenry as a collective body, and the individual. There was a clear separation of function, however. The idea that the state does not have a crucial function in providing for the general welfare or that the church can be an arm of the state in this respect involves an altering of the classical covenant, altering also the relationship of the citizenry to the state on the one hand and to the religious community on the other.

Precisely because the state must provide for the general welfare and the religious community must hold the state accountable in this role, there is much at stake in the quality of the relationships between parts of the religious community. Just how does the religious community uphold its covenantal obligations vis-à-vis the state? Certainly it does so by affirming the deep connections that bind together people of faith in an embedded unity, because that is the presupposition of those obligations. But just as certainly it cannot do so without maintaining a critical distance from the state — a kind of subversiveness as it were, which subjects the state to a thorough testing as to its own obligations. The latter follows from the former.

Theocentric vs. Christocentric Theologies in Community Ministry

The executive director of a community ministry in Louisville, Kentucky, proposed that the ministry expand its circle of Christian congregations to include the synagogues in their urban neighborhood. Earlier, this ministry had broken new ground in ecumenical relations by formulating a covenant in which all the congregations had joined. This covenant was distinguished by the inclusion of a statement of mutual recognition of the sacrament of baptism in each and all of the member congregations. Every baptized person was to receive a copy of this covenant at the time of his or her baptism. Yet, although the document was a step forward ecumenically, it was a barrier to interfaith participation because of its specifically Christian orientation, including a statement about unity "in Christ." It contributed to the defeat of the proposal of the executive director.

Juan Luis Segundo addresses the above dilemma: "The real problem of Christian unity in my opinion, comes down to this: When will we manage to break that conservative, oppressive, undifferentiated unity of Christians in order to establish an open dialogue with all those, be they Christian or not, who are committed to the historical liberation that should serve as the basis for the 'service of reconciliation' in and through justice"?[32]

From our standpoint, the general applicability of theistic covenant thought makes it particularly appropriate as a basis for a theology of local interfaith and ecumenical community ministry. Even in a ministry that is composed exclusively of Christian congregations, a christological basis (such as the concept of the Body of Christ) might have divisive potential. Furthermore, if and when congregations agree on a stated christological basis, the circle is immediately closed to persons of other religious convictions who might want to join in this essentially public ministry.[33]

Segundo's point is that insofar as the Christian social project includes the liberation of the oppressed, it does not have to have the name of Christ imprinted on it in order for it to be valid. Nor does the work of a community ministry have to be done in the name of Christ to be valid — anymore than giving bread to a hungry person requires the stamp of Christ on the bread (as some have suggested) in order for the act to be truly efficacious.

Repairing the Broken Covenant (III): Points of Departure

In light of the above, the following touchstones commend themselves to our movement:

- The local community, with its various expressions of faith, is itself charged with revelatory significance. An embedded unity of people of faith becomes realizable in response to the needs of the local community. An ecumenical theology that is not grounded in experience and active involvement "at the most local level possible" must be held suspect.

- Any theology that seriously takes into account the potential and actual depth of interfaith and ecumenical relationships at the local level will almost certainly have a distinctly countercultural cast. It will be a radical theology in every sense of the word, even if it does not intend to be such; going to the roots and affecting all else — finding God in the intersection of faiths and in the common action that ensues.

- An ecumenical theology that results in building higher barriers between Christianity and other faiths does not sufficiently take into account the given interrelationship of all of creation and all of humanity; and it must be considered inappropriate for the time and world in which we live. There is plenty of warrant in scripture, tradition, and experience for a theistic theology that traces indissoluble triadic relationships beginning with local interfaith and ecumenical unity and ending in the fulfillment of God's good purposes for humanity and Earth.

Chapter 4

From Local to Global and Back

The Pilgrimage of Local Interfaith and Ecumenical Ministry

The connections that give life don't just sit and wait; they move. They themselves are alive because they are human. They move because they are on their way to something new that doesn't quite exist yet. More accurately they would argue that it lives in the mind of God and in the faith of those who follow God. Far from resisting the future, they feel beckoned by God toward opportunities.[1]

As an advocate of faith-inspired local health coalitions, "deep connectedness" is Gunderson's way of acknowledging the "embedded unity" that is the foundation of community ministry. We have traced the trajectory of this connectedness or unity as it moves from a cluster of local congregations (chapter 1) to the larger circle of the local body politic (chapter 2) to the still wider and trans-local scene of interfaith relations (chapter 3). Now we come to explore the global aspect of this spiral.

Each year a few community ministries engage in a hospitality program during the holidays called Christmas

International House (CIH). Lasting relationships that transcend the boundaries of faith communities and nations have resulted from this program. In one instance the author accepted the invitation of an Armenian student to visit her family in Jerusalem, where he learned much about that tradition and about Jerusalem that he otherwise would not have known. In another instance, the program hosted Iranian students while their government was holding Americans hostage (1980). The program also hosted a young man in the first wave of those who came to study in the United States from the People's Republic of China. On a more lighthearted note but of poignant significance for the future, Japanese students had to be discouraged from reverently drinking of the "sacred" but polluted stream that flowed past the birthplace of Abraham Lincoln!

When community ministry experiences and affirms, understands and accepts its given local relationships of unity, it inevitably touches the larger contexts of faith and humanity. The Dutch missiologist L. A. Hoedemaker traces and describes a chronology of Protestant missions, which has parallels in local ecumenical mission in the United States. He posits three successive stages: (1) the eschatology of conquest, (2) the eschatology of rivalry, and (3) the eschatology of unity. As the eschatology of conquest meant conquering the world for Christ, ecumenical mission in the nineteenth-century United States meant cooperation in conquering the untamed wilderness of the West for Christ. As the twentieth-century eschatology of rivalry brought grand coalitions to promote and demonstrate an alternative worldview in the face of secularization, local ecumenical mission in the United States took exactly that same tack. Now, ecumenical/interfaith community ministry heralds a new era that anticipates Hoedemaker's call for an eschatology of unity by building alliances on a local scale that eventually will have a global impact.

Globalization as we now experience it is a distorted version of the realization of this eschatology of the unity of humankind: it promises a kind of universal convergence of economic interests. What its exponents tend to hide or downplay is an increasing disparity and conflict between rich and poor, between the few and the many, between global uniformity and global plurality, as well as a merciless attack on the natural environment and on the efficacy of local, democratic politics. These issues, in my opinion, assure that the quest for a true unity of humankind will reassert itself beyond all accomplishments of "globalization" understood strictly in terms of laissez-faire economics.[2]

Seen in the light of the problems of "globalization," the value of the embedded unity of local congregations lies in modeling, upholding, and pursuing an authentic kind of connectedness — one that ultimately embraces all of creation and humankind. It welcomes "the world" into its local purview naturally, much as did the local ecumenical holiday hospitality program (above). The promise of community ministry lies in its potential to forge a truly new type of ecumenical and interfaith mission that focuses on the unity of humankind in sustainable local communities. This is a journey that begins and ends in the neighborhoods and small towns and rural counties of the world.

Journey to Earth

A community ministry that embarked on a project to build government-subsidized housing for the elderly and handicapped encountered intense opposition from the neighborhood because the project was to be built on a ball field that had long been a favorite place of recreation. The dispute had to be settled by litigation. Another ministry joined a community organization in its attempt to prevent airport expansion from destroying a neighborhood. When the effort failed, it started a housing corporation to build houses for some who had to relocate because of the planned expansion. The problem of community ministry in respect to environmental issues is that it tends to be somewhat myopic about Earth, defining problems and solutions entirely in terms of its own "turf." Yet, community ministry has great potential in regard to environmental issues because it operates at a juncture where economic development, social policy, human development, and ecological concerns meet in a local matrix.

Some of the earliest community ministries were involved in the first Earth Day observances of the 1970s. My observation is that their most visible ecological activity since then has taken the form of gardening. One urban ministry has a large plot on the edge of a city for the use of city residents who want and need space for gardening. Another does urban gardening, cultivating urban lots and using them to provide fresh produce to augment a food pantry. Two others, an inner-city ministry and one located in a suburb, have joined forces to market farm products from the rim of the city in the city itself — thus establishing a mutually advantageous economic relationship.

If we think of the surface of Earth as one organ, say an epidermis, we can more easily grasp the idea of an organic, Earth link among local communities. Just as the epidermis is one single organ, the whole of which may be affected by a disturbance anywhere on the body, the health of Earth is determined by the aggregate health of small, discrete locations or communities. Yet because each community is located on the same "epidermis" as all others, it must be concerned as well with the health of all the others. The question, then, is: just what would be involved when the well-being of an urban neighborhood or other local community also contributes to the health of the entire planet? Interdependence requires that each community become aware of how it relates to and depends upon the piece of Earth for which it is most responsible — its plant and animal life, its natural resources and beauty. By getting "closer" to the part of Earth with which it lives, each community better understands the common bond and interest it has with the other communities of Earth. Therefore we speak of a journey to Earth in every place.

An oft-repeated and viewed image of our day is that of Pope John Paul II stooping to kiss the ground after stepping from a plane — formerly his first official gesture as he arrived in a country to pay a visit. There is a symbolism here that reaches far beyond its intended meaning. What the pope may have intended was to honor a particular country by honoring the soil that it claims as its own, a diplomatic gesture that implies there is much in the culture, history, and national spirit of the country that is pleasing in God's (and the pope's) sight. It may be worth pointing out, however, that no matter where the pope travels, it is the same Earth that he visits in every place. By performing the same gesture no matter where he went, he not only acknowledged the particularity of each place; he also signified its connectedness to every other place. He could well be interpreted as saying, "Not only is this country important, but this whole Earth is of first importance in every place."

For all of the ineluctable and revelatory significance of the most local level, it would be an inadmissible contradiction to say that our caring for its diverse humanity, life, and nature stops here. It only begins here. Yet there is no justification for "skipping over" the local any more in the local/global political sense than on the local/global religious scene (chapter 3, above).

Just as one's interfaith and ecumenical commitments on a global level must remain suspect so long as one is not engaged locally, one's commitment to sustainable community globally is meaningless unless one delivers on that commitment locally. The very term "sustainable community" implies that our local communities are the points of departure for a healthy planet. This term is offered as an alternative to the term "sustainable development" for discerning what is truly involved in assuring the survival of Earth and its peoples. But the substitution of "community" for "development" has no meaning unless we experience community concretely in places where face-to-face relationships nurture it.[3] Thus, community ministry always performs global as well as local tasks; but it must perform them all locally.

The Covenant in Creation

An informal survey of some of the largest and best-known community ministries revealed that, aside from involvement in shaping public transportation plans, pooling transportation resources, and several variations on the theme of gardening, community ministry has not advocated much on behalf of Earth. We have been slow to acknowledge that the given, covenantal relationships among local congregations make them accountable for their relationship to Earth as well as to the local civil community. Larry Rasmussen's words do convict us.

> For if the incarnation of God is a matter of stipulated time and place ("In the fifteenth year of the reign of Tiberius, when Pontius Pilate was governor of Judea, and Herod was ruler of Galilee . . ."); and if the way of God is a matter of earthen vessels and spirited flesh ("the word of God came to John, son of Zechariah in the wilderness," Luke 3:1–2), then it rests firmly with the faith community to discern the movement of its own incumbent age and fashion living wisdom from the clay of its own appointed earth.[4]

In her compelling interpretation of Genesis 1–11, Dutch biblical scholar Ellen van Wolde[5] points out that Genesis 2 and 3 develop the idea of an essential relationship between human being and Earth. God made human being because "there was not yet human being to cultivate the earth" (2:5). God made human being (and the animals of the field) "from the stuff of the earth" (2:7). The first things that God does after making human being are to plant a garden, into which God places human being (2:8), and to make trees grow from the earth (2:9). Then, Genesis 4:1–16 shows that the relationship between human being and the earth is dependent upon the quality of relationship among human beings, as between one strong human being (Cain) and his weak fellow human being (Abel). When Cain kills Abel, the voice of the blood of Abel cries out from the earth. Cain is cursed from the earth. When he cultivates the earth, it will no longer yield him its strength but he will be a fugitive and wanderer over it. Then, in 4:26, people begin to call on God using the unpronounceable name — YHWH. "The relationship of YHWH-earth-human being, man-woman, and human being-fellow human being thus becomes a totality of reciprocal relationships."[6]

The cause of the great flood was that human being violated the web of reciprocity, affecting all of these relationships. "The earth was destroyed before God's face and the earth was filled with violence. . . . All living beings destroyed their way on the earth. And God said to Noah: the end of all living beings stands before my eyes. . . . Look, I shall destroy them from the earth" (6:11–13, van Wolde's translation). Then, when the flood is over and the curse is removed,

> It is not so much human beings that are rescued but the earth. The earth continues to be dependent on human beings for its cultivation, but the ongoing existence of the earth and all living beings is detached from, or made independent of, the actions of human beings, good and bad. . . . The law of the succession of the seasons and days will impose its rhythm on generations of human beings. It is the time of the earth that counts.[7]

In the light of this analysis we explain evil in the world and wickedness of human being not so much by disobedience toward God (as in the paradise story) but rather by the unfaithfulness of human beings to Earth, and to other human beings and the animals. Genesis 4, the story of the murder of Abel by his brother Cain, and Genesis 9, the aftermath of the great flood, describe the failure of human being to recognize and respect the principle of life in all living creatures.[8] Finally, the climax of the creation stories is God's offer of a renewed covenant — a second chance — with the word "covenant" appearing seven times in 9:8–17. Each time the word is used it refers to three relationships — God and Noah, God and all living beings, God and Earth (although throughout history this passage has been read as a covenant only between God and Noah with his descendants). "Noah and his descendants constitute an important part of the living beings of the earth, but they form part of a greater whole. The bow in the sky spans the earth and protects it. It points both to the autonomy of the earth and to the bond between God and the earth. Now that the earth has been washed clean of human faults and shortcomings by a great flood, God wants to protect and guarantee its ongoing existence."[9]

Interfaith and ecumenical community ministry finds itself in a position to model a reciprocity of relationships that includes the claims of Earth on a local scale. In fact when one considers the extent of the threat to Earth and its nonhuman inhabitants, history's judgment on community ministry may depend on how well it learns this lesson and acts upon it.

The "Earth Charter" (March 2000) calls upon the peoples of the Earth to "declare our responsibility to one another, to the greater community of life, and to the future generations. . . . Earth, our home is alive with a unique community of life. . . . The protection of Earth's vitality, diversity, and beauty is a sacred trust. . . . The choice is ours: form a global partnership to care for Earth and one another or risk the destruction of ourselves and diversity of life."[10] In these phrases we recognize those given, triadic relationships of interdependence and mutual responsibility that are always the mark and result of covenant thinking. Among the "interdependent principles for a sustainable way of life" advocated by the Charter are the strengthening of local communities so they may provide better care for their environments.

Journey to the People

A needs assessment in one community revealed a need for more child-care services for single-parent families and for two-parent families where both worked full-time. The community ministry there mobilized the local community and, with the help of state and county grants, local church funds, and loans, built and opened two state-of-the-art child-care facilities — one in the middle of its small city and one in a rural part of the county. Both facilities housed other, supplementary, services and agencies. Both served a population that included lower- through middle-class working families. As the facilities were being constructed, federal and state regulations shifted imperceptibly in favor of franchised, private, for-profit, regionally based child-care corporations. Such corporations opened facilities that competed with those that were generated locally — especially for families that could pay the full, unsubsidized fees. Because they were private, for-profit corporations that did not depend upon and often refused to accept subsidized clients, they found ways to sidestep the high (and costly standards) of government certifying agencies. As a result, the community ministry child-care program eventually faced the choice of either closing or turning over the operation to governmental or quasi-government agencies. The result is that almost all child care in that community is now administered on a regional basis by either the governmental or business sectors, and the children of the unemployed and working poor of the community are effectively separated from the children of the upward mobile classes. This trend has affected hundreds of local nonprofit child-care programs throughout the United States.

As responsible community ministry journeys to its "own appointed earth," it joins itself to all the inhabitants of Earth. As the problem of child-care in a relatively prosperous North American community demonstrates, these realities include the economic juggernaut of "globalization," the impact and victims of which are found in every local community, with the exception of fortress enclaves for the very rich. The common struggle against the incursions of globalization may be the single most important factor in connecting local communities for the good of each community. The Earth Charter (above) views local community as a sign of hope and a potential source of resistance to forces destructive of Earth; while "globalization," as we now experience it, stands for those forces that threaten not only Earth but also local community, Earth's best defense.

Globalization, knows no "local"; its "local" is really "regional"! For example, whereas a community ministry in Rochester, New York, may view its neighborhood as "local," globalization asks that we view an entire region composed of, say, Rochester and Buffalo and, in some scenarios, even Toronto, as "local." The "neighborhood" suddenly and eerily expands far beyond the ken and daily interaction of the masses of people whose "local" contains notions of proximity and daily life. Decision-making power is ceded to regional economic entities in the name of becoming more competitive in world markets. Relatively trivial decisions are left to elected municipal officials. Business conglomerates and colluding state or other regional authorities control decision-making on a global and regional basis and supersede (by one means or another) local progressive environmental and labor practices that are the result of literally hundreds of years of hard-fought political battles.

Where the above does not already describe the reality, it lies in the foreseeable future of every local community if trends continue. These trends are pushed along by global, corporation-controlled, undemocratic economic organizations, such as the International Monetary Fund (IMF), the World Bank (WB), and the World Trade Organization (WTO), whose policies are engines of globalization, regionalization, and corporate hegemony. The IMF and WB now determine the political decisions of whole nations (not to mention local communities) through restrictions they place on international financial aid and credit. These restrictions result in an ever-deepening spiral of debt and actually stipulate the reduction of essential budgets for health, education, housing, and the environment — actions that are tantamount to the sundering of local communities.

Because we invest this local level with revelatory and theological significance, we cannot avoid treating globalization as a subject for sober theological reflection. Major programmatic funding sources such as United Way, foundations, and governments are beginning to require institutional resources that go far beyond the capacity of most community ministries and all nonprofit organizations that seek to operate on a truly local scale. These requirements assume an organization of regional rather than local scope, possessing operating fund surpluses to protect against cash-flow variances (in an earlier day, surpluses were an anathema), large-scale public fund-raising (whereas, in contrast, community ministry finances are, in the first instance, an extension of local congregational budgets), public relations expertise, highly articulated financial management, compliance monitoring, data collection personnel — without which even a neighborhood organization is deemed substandard at best and irresponsible at worst.

Increasingly (and ironically from our viewpoint) local religious institutions feel they must transform themselves into the size or scale that mirrors or competes with globalizing institutions. A community ministry that I directed several years ago operated on an annual budget of $1,300,000, which was already several times larger than that of the average local ministry. At that time I estimated that if this ministry wanted to maintain its current program and conform to all the organizational standards of the new (regional) economy, it would have to, in fact, expand its program and administrative capacity to a level and a budget of approximately $7,000,000! Thus, the demands of scale are leading to developments in social ministry and the nonprofit sector generally that have been occurring for many years already in the world of business — consolidation and merger. This problem of scale applies to every community ministry in the country, whether in an agricultural county or urban neighborhood.

A community ministry composed of some ten congregations had to curtail its activities and programs when most of its member churches began to lose members to a fast-growing megachurch in the area. These congregations responded to the threat by imitating the megachurch — leading to more of a competitive than cooperative spirit among them, leading to the building of competing and underused, gymnasium-sized "family life centers," and reduced resources for either local or global mission.

The (for the most part) antiecumenical/interfaith and antilocal-scale megachurches of ten to twenty thousand–plus members arise, wholly uncritical of and even willingly shaped by the forces and ideology of globalization. In general, they tout the global/regional scale and evidence little or no commitment to local community as such. Yet they make claims on public resources on behalf of a reactionary social agenda, which they would see attached to the globalization processes. The real challenge of the megachurch is that it is a regional rather than local entity. It simulates local scale by encouraging the formation of small groups within its huge membership — much as a regional shopping mall may try to simulate the local by developing bogus "neighborhoods" of shops. In all these megainstitutions we are faced with the specter of "virtual" local community rather than the real political, economic, social, and cultural thing.[11]

Herein lie challenges to community ministry: To what extent can we negotiate the demands of scale and still remain responsive to the needs of our local communities, including the very need to survive? How can we be true to the covenant mandate to work ecumenically in these communities? Is it realistic to think that we can maintain these ministries under the pressures of globalization? Thus, the urgency of Lukas Vischer's question:

> Having transcended the boundaries of space and time, how can human beings find their way back to an emphasis on the local community? ... The dynamic force of present processes is so strong that movements of opposition seem to have little chance. The consensus on which it relies seems so evident that it can be presented as the only realistic course. Proposals in other directions can be dismissed as nostalgia, romantic dreams, or idealistic programmes, of academic interest perhaps but not applicable in reality.[12]

Vischer raises the same questions about local community as I do about community ministry, and it could well be that the last line of resistance against the forces of globalization in the local community is community ministry. Because of its implicit belief in the ultimacy of local community, ecumenical and interfaith community ministry may be, under certain circumstances, in a position to mobilize the forces of resistance.

The country saw a preview of the capacity for resistance of local ecumenical coalitions in the late 1970s when Big Steel abandoned its mills in and around Youngstown, Ohio. The story is related by a United Church of Christ minister, Chuck Rawlings, in an article entitled "The Global Economy's Opening Hand: The Steel Shut Down." He writes,

"How the crisis in Youngstown was precipitated, its underlying causes slowly identified, and ecumenical resistance
mobilized for the sake of the community is a morality play
of historic proportions. In it can be seen not only the reach
of corporate and financial power but also how the argument
advanced by the world of business seeks to elevate business
decision-making beyond moral criticism."[13]

In a real sense, the theology of community ministry
that we advance in this essay will be tested in the cru-
cible of globalization. Unfortunately for our purposes, the
antilocal ideology of globalization has some currency in the
religious community itself. Vischer cites the glowing opti-
mism of Michael Camdessus, then general director of the
International Monetary Fund while addressing a group of
Roman Catholic intellectuals on the future "global city." In
his speech, Camdessus regards all the signs of globalization as "harbingers of a new order — a unified world and a
world economy which provides a home to all." Vischer sees
the churches as divided on the issue and he anticipates a
theological debate soon to come.[14]

Globalization and the ideology of "free trade" derived
much initial credibility among faith communities partly
because of positive associations with the word *agora*, or marketplace, in Greek. More than one community ministry of
the 1960s, when it located near or in a regional shopping
mall, used the term *agora* to signify a dimension other than
the purely commercial. They invoked the New Testament
image of Paul preaching in the *agora* of Athens, and the
agora was understood as a medium for global interchange
and understanding — much as were the commercial centers
and fairs of the sixteenth and seventeenth centuries — Ams-
terdam, Antwerp, the Hanseatic League, etc. This was trade
that could liberate in the sense of promoting new ideas and
encouraging acceptance of hitherto-unknown cultures; but
it was anything but free trade in the sense of being unregulated, where economic life is not rooted in specific localities
or subject to political structures — as is increasingly the case

with our globalized, corporation-dominated *agora*. Thus, if community ministry is to rise to the challenge of globalization, it will have to own and articulate certain more or less new theological perspectives. One, according to Vischer, has to do with the importance of communion at the local level, which is his acknowledgment of the embedded unity that we have posited among local institutional expressions of faith.[15] Community ministry must insist on the importance of communion at the local level as inherently good and essential to building mutually accountable relations at every level.

In the American context, even our child of the Enlightenment, Thomas Jefferson, regarded the local community as the linchpin of political accountability in a democracy, and he actually reflected on this point theologically. As did so many others in the American political tradition, Jefferson juxtaposed the terms "community" and "covenant," visualizing "community" on a small enough scale to maximize political participation and "covenant" in terms of divine maintenance of that American experiment in localism.[16]

Finally, following Vischer, local churches must defend the interests of the local community against the claims of overarching universal structures. The theological task of contributing to the building of local community, therefore, leads to the societal task of resisting the concentrations of power and to the social mission of defending local community against universal claims. One pursues this theology and these efforts not exclusively on behalf of local community, but essentially on behalf of responsible community at all levels, because a sustainable and just humanity Earth-wide rests on sustainable and just local communities.

Given that the forces opposed to the survival of sustainable and just local communities are formidable, the internal logic of which is driving the destruction of Earth's biological and sociological bases of local community, we must ask whether the course of history can still be changed. Are clusters of local churches willing to pay the price of joining in or leading the effort? Interfaith/ecumenical community ministry organizations might be the means by which the churches can shape the beginnings of an alternative, more courageous, more determined approach than we have witnessed heretofore.

Homecoming

I speak of a return to what I would call "our true place of origin" — not our ancestral or tribal lands, not the place of our birth and childhood, not necessarily where our roots once grew deepest, but to where we are called in this moment, where each day we are re-created anew by the community, its creatures, its Earth, its relationships, its responsibilities, and its potentialities.

Our journeys to Earth and its peoples have made us aware of how vulnerable our true place of origin is. We must raise the dikes against the threatening flood. We are called to resist the tidal waves of indifferent and unregulated capital that would obliterate our communities and Earth that sustains them. At the very least we are called to resist an ethos of competition that would pit the congregations of the community against each other instead of uniting them on behalf of the whole community. Instead, under a restored covenant, congregations are called to put their unity at the service of local community, which, although threatened by decisions made in distant boardrooms, is itself a source of divine revelation for us — something not to be defended halfheartedly. We are called to resist any attempt to unlink political/theological discourse, trivializing politics and disarming theology.

We also resist the tendency to make ecumenical and interfaith relations purely a matter of global negotiations and transactions between supraterrestrial authorities, while the crucial struggles are taking place in our local communities. For example, we need ministries that know to combat hunger and homelessness by working for economic and racial justice. We need ministries that work for an authentic local unity — ministries that work toward an inclusive community of diverse knowledges so that many local human resources may be enlisted in the struggle against undemocratic, antilocal and laissez-faire forms of globalization.

With Aruna Gnanadason, we ask: "In a context of globalization can the ecumenical movement not provide an alternative vision which would stress our global interdependence and then leave it to each community, in its own place, to work out what citizenship in an ecumenical earth requires of us?" Thus, we must nurture relationships among people of faith locally and globally so that, as they deepen, they increase our capacity to resist thralldom to local cultural norms where they support forces of domination and oppression.[17]

The Vulnerability of Local Community Today

In the late 1980s a group calling itself "LOVE Inc.," with headquarters in Holland, Michigan, attempted to globalize the field of community ministry by establishing franchises around the country. Based on an exclusively Christian theology, these congregation-based franchises were to follow priorities generated not by the communities they were serving but by the headquarters staff. They developed uniform materials that would guide each franchise in its work. The assumption was that even for community ministry, the differences between localities were not of great significance.

It is abundantly clear how vulnerable our local communities and ministries are in the face of globalizing tendencies. The amounts of capital funds potentially available for buying out local businesses are huge — large enough so that literally no locally based corporation, no matter how large, is immune. Just this increasing possibility of the buyout of a local company loosens the ties of that company to the local community. It only takes a parenthetical, under-the-breath phrase by the CEO of the company at a Rotary luncheon to make the entire community fearful. The buyout results in the loss of jobs and control by local persons and the possible reduction or even cessation of operations locally in favor of other locations. But the incentives needed to retain a company or to find a replacement may be equally devastating. For example, localities might grant the company significant tax abatement — thereby reducing the capacity of the community to provide essential public services. The company might be permitted to uproot and eliminate whole neighborhoods or destroy ecologically important wetlands or other of Earth's resources that nourish life and sustain local community. It might be allowed certain labor practices and reduction of wages and benefits to an extent that formerly would have been unthinkable.

Furthermore, large retail corporations, through franchising and establishing local outlets, subvert and displace the small, often family-run businesses that help to maintain a sense of place and community in each neighborhood or locality. With impunity they will locate near the locally run businesses and, with the capital needed to temporarily undercut the prices of their competitor, they will make the older establishment economically untenable. In recent years the nonprofit sector has been a target. In the 1970s the Singer Corporation unsuccessfully attempted to become the dominant provider of child-care programs through the establishment of franchised operations throughout the country. Although they failed, the field has essentially been privatized and regionalized for all children but those requiring subsidization (see p. 83 above). The integrity of whole denominations may be affected by invasions of large amounts of TNC-related funding with a particular social agenda.[18]

In a sense, this is, by now, an old story — the destruction of the patently local by behemoth economic forces. The conservative churchman Jan H. Boer, in a chapter entitled "Squeezing Out Local People and Enterprise," begins his description with the Standard Oil Company of the United States in the 1870s before moving to the international scene and our own day.[19] Yet, in our day this oft-described phenomenon has taken on unprecedented dimensions of speed and size. For those who regard local community as essential for the sustainability of Earth and its people, the alarm has sounded. Already, in certain parts of the world, communities of indigenous peoples are facing extinction. The question arises: can sustainability be achieved within the framework of the present economic system? In asking the question, Julio de Santa Ana, agreeing with Larry Rasmussen, questions the use of the term "sustainable development" because it may be taken to imply an easy affirmative to the question. He wants people of faith in particular to consider whether some fundamental changes in the present trend are indicated.

De Santa Ana identifies the underlying forces of globalization that result in the concrete economic vulnerability described above. These forces include the communications technology that encourages virtual relationships as opposed to personal, identity-strengthening interactions in the public sphere. They also involve the imposition of mass culture and homogenization of patterns of life, which obstruct a community's links to its own culture and depersonalize the human relationships within it. At the most basic level lie two realities, which are devastating to local community: The first is what de Santa Ana calls "the instrumental intention of economic activities," which refers to the unexamined, unintended consequences of economic policy, the reduction of most created beings to means to an end, and the "amputation" of a living tie to the environment. The second is the prevailing notion that only one global economic paradigm is valid for every local community — a "one size fits all" approach to which all cultures must adjust, which has been characterized by the French phrase, "la pensée unique."

As we have noted, faith-based social projects are not above the strategy of "la pensée unique."[20]

Repairing the Broken Covenant (IV) — Mobilizing Theological Resources to Preserve Local Community

In 1993, the Robert Wood Johnson Foundation initiated a program called "Faith in Action" by which local coalitions of churches could apply for grants that would concentrate on mobilizing volunteers in programs for chronically ill older adults. Already operating groups were not eligible to apply for grants. Since then, millions of dollars have been poured into local communities, provided that faith-based coalitions form and focus their energies for the single purpose of the Robert Wood Johnson Foundation's "Faith in Action" program. The Foundation had discovered what their literature refers to as the "latent" energy of faith-based local coalitions, and it set about to exploit it for their unquestionably laudable purposes.

Precisely because of the commendable goals of this program, it provides a challenging opportunity to present a theological critique of a network that became a competitor to existing ecumenical/interfaith community ministry groups in numerous local settings.

On the Meaning and Purpose of Embedded Local Unity

When the literature of the Johnson Foundation refers to "latent" potential in the various local faith communities, it is a tacit recognition of the embedded unity of local congregations of which we have spoken in this book. According to our understanding, embedded unity is a gift to be used on behalf of the local community. The people of faith are accountable to God in their relationships to each other, to the community, and to their part of Earth. In this concrete situation of day-to-day relationships, they have the Great Commandment as their guide (to love God and to love the neighbor). Because it is God who makes these relationships of unity and accountability, it is only from this matrix that responsible action derives. Such action is truly faith in action — that is, faith that unites the believer with other believers in accountability to God for her/his actions vis-à-vis the neighbor and community. Clearly, "Faith in Action" of the Johnson Foundation does not use the term "faith" in our sense of the word because it does not acknowledge the local faith community and the local community as the point of departure. It does not have an authentic theological relationship to the community or to its churches. It merely seeks to use the energies of the local faith community for its own purposes, however praiseworthy they may be.

On the Morally Indivisible Character of the Reciprocal Relations among People of Faith in the Local Community

The goal of the "Faith in Action" program — to mobilize volunteers on behalf of the health of chronically ill older adults — is truly praiseworthy on our very own terms. It may be seen, as theologians often have seen it, as an extension of the commandment, "honor your father and your mother." The promise that accompanies the commandment, however ("that your days may be long in the land which the Holy One, your God gives you"), connects the specific injunction to the health and peace of creation. The commandment encapsulates global/local and Earth/humanity connections in responsible local action. Therefore we ask: how does the Faith and Action program relate to the claims of Earth in each community (the "land" in which God promises long life); to the claims of justice in relation to the general treatment of older persons; to the failings of health systems that affect both the older and general population? Insofar as "Faith in Action" does not address these issues it is immoral because it distracts from related moral claims in favor of a narrow focus on one.

Dealing with moral claims in fragmented ways contributes to disunity in the community of faith and in the community at large. The local community as a whole, not some single aspect of it, is to be "a city set upon a hill." Here a tremendous burden has been placed on the local faith community; and it cannot be executed except in a deeply unified, nonfragmented way. For example, in relation to the problem of the widening gap between the rich and the poor, it is our task, as Paul Hanson says, to imitate the example of a benevolent, compassionate God by demonstrating that there is enough for all on this earth if people live simply and generously. If the faith community is unified in this basic approach to life, then it is at least a little more likely that the sharp divisions between the "haves" and the "have-nots" in the human family will be healed.[21]

On the Divine Mandate and Calling of Local Communities to Resist Systems of Domination

The "Faith in Action" program does not question why certain groups in our society never reach the age where "Faith in Action" volunteers might be helpful for them. When one walks the streets of many "developing nations" (or poor communities in the United States), one sees very few senior adults, if any, because of the low average life expectancy in such places. Yet there is not the faintest hint in the literature or practice of Faith in Action that there might be some merit in resisting current trends and practices in our society not only on behalf of older adults but also on behalf of those who, because of poverty, racism, and lack of health care, are unlikely ever to become older adults. It is revealing, moreover, that Faith in Action literature does not make any reference to the local body politic except for notice of endorsements by politicians and government officials — as if their programs would operate in a political vacuum. Covenantal perspectives on ecumenical/interfaith community ministry, however, make it a matter of divine mandate that ecumenical unity and interfaith cooperation find concrete expression in local politics.

Make no mistake: beneath the placid tableau of volunteers bringing meals to the homebound, there is a recurring struggle taking place in every local community against the forces of nihilism and oppression — a struggle that would be uneven were it not for the divine compassionate pledge to save Earth and humanity. Ecumenical/interfaith community ministry acts against the backdrop of this struggle and in response to this pledge. A liberated community ministry makes itself and the community aware of injustice and violence to Earth and its creaturely inhabitants. Because of the divine promise, and trusting in it, community ministry dares to ask and presses the body politic to ask: "How can we begin to form redeemed communities that are characterized by both justice and non-violence?" (Albrecht; see p. 35 above). The most problematic aspect of the "Faith in Action" program is that it actually militates against the raising of this question because it is not in a position to propose an agenda that is specific to any given local community. Yet, in our view, one will find in any local community the matrices of relationships from which revolutionary solutions might emerge. The responsible stance of the people of faith in the political arena is the prophetic one that opposes greed, special privilege, and inequalities, and looks toward an alternative vision of justice and peace.[22]

On the Principle of Subsidiarity and an Alternative Globalization

Maria Carmelita de Freitas speaks of "the religion of the market" and its consequence, "the logic of exclusion," whereby something far worse than the reduction of resources for social services is taking place. "It is the abandonment of the poor to themselves, the lack of commitment on the part of the State to the social sector."[23]

Yet she does not despair but calls upon local religious communities to deploy their imagination and talents in countering this relatively new crisis in relations between the powerful and the weak. In the same vein, Robert Schreiter puts forward the idea that globalization has actually heightened the sense of the local and has made interfaith relations more important at every level, including especially the local.[24]

Anthony Giddens goes a step further than Schreiter to say that globalization is the reason for the revival of local cultural identities insofar as it has weakened national identities. He sees some potentially enhancing aspects of globalization in local daily life in the examples of instant electronic communication and greater equality of women and men. While granting the problematic nature of untrammeled "free trade" that characterizes globalization for many, he points out that the "shell institutions" created by globalization, among them the nation-state, may no longer be adequate to the tasks they are called upon to perform.[25]

Although I do not agree with Roland Robertson that "local" is, at root, a relative term (see Introduction), it is most helpful for our purposes to hear globalization described as a compression of the world resulting in the linking (but not necessarily the homogenization) of localities; or to hear of a world culture that is constituted by an interconnectedness of local cultures. Robertson is persuaded that local cultures necessarily have much more of a role to play vis-à-vis globalization than has been acknowledged heretofore in the debate.[26]

All of the above encourages us to suggest that the problem is not so much how to hold back the tide of globalization as it is how to identify and support an appropriate strategy for the forces of localization. Local interfaith and ecumenical community ministry may have a role in maximizing this effort.

In the search for theological resources and tools, we will find at least one just waiting to be taken up — the principle of subsidiarity. Larry Rasmussen mentions it as the basis of the ideal of "sustainable community." What is the principle of subsidiarity? The definition in Webster's New Third International Dictionary refers to a theory in sociology: "Functions which subordinate or local organizations perform effectively belong more properly to them than to a dominant central organization." In *Earth Community, Earth Ethics,* Rasmussen elevates subsidiarity to the status of "one of the moral norms of sustainability" and broadens the definition by specifying the importance of place and scale. "The key is appropriate scale and action."[27]

This test may admit of actions on a global scale, such as an international project to restore the ozone layer in the atmosphere, but it may also mean dismantling certain controlling global structures in favor of local ones — those having to do with food and shelter, for example. It gives impetus as well to local, participatory democracy insofar as the full energies of local communities cannot be effectuated merely by commandeering them — as Faith in Action would seem to do. The Faith in Action program would do better to encourage global actions for which, as the child of a global corporation, it is better suited — perhaps to form a global interfaith coalition to advocate on behalf of seniors.

Thus, an alternative globalization, one shaped by the principle of subsidiarity, comes into view. It preserves an appropriately large space for self-determination and hence sustainability of local communities. It does not compromise their capacity to fulfill their own particular covenanted responsibilities before God as they understand them. It does not prevent them from seeing the issues and problems of their community as made of whole cloth that must be tackled as such. Nor does it compromise the capacity of local communities to resist domination by outside forces. We in interfaith and ecumenical community ministry would do well to "baptize" such a globalization and work toward it in our respective neighborhoods.

Chapter 5

Toward the Beloved Community

How then can we, as part of the dominant [group or class], begin to form redeemed communities characterized by both justice and nonviolence?

— Gloria Albrecht,
The Character of Our Communities

In any theology of community ministry, the "beloved community" must be an ecumenical and interfaith process that engages the body politic. It represents the potentiality of the local body politic were it to function properly — that is, according to the mandates and insights afforded by a transcendent and inclusive covenant among humanity in that place. A principle of resistance resides in this properly functioning local body politic that may itself become a counterforce within and an antidote to the dominant community. The question we put forward is this: what are the characteristics of this properly functioning body politic theologically understood?[1]

Covenant-Inspired Politics and Community Ministry — A Symbiosis

A community ministry in Fairhope, Alabama, decided to try to do something about the systematic withholding of public services to the predominantly African American rural communities on the outskirts of town — in spite of the fact that their residents were taxed for services. The mostly white churches of this ministry formed an alliance with the predominantly African American congregations of the area. The ecumenical ministry gave financial support for a local person willing to be trained as a community organizer. This alliance was successful in its first objective — to have the streets of the community paved.

Local community organization is an important part of community ministry because, at its best, it uses the principle of resistance in mobilizing a part of the community to the end that the entire community and its processes will better exhibit the beloved community of which we speak. Church-based community organization provides an opportunity for local congregations to practice resistance in the dominant community, building up the sinews of the beloved community. For example, some local communities have found a way to resist the powerful National Rifle Association (NRA) by enacting local gun-control laws. Thus they were able to curtail violence in their communities without recourse to state and national legislatures, which were essentially in the pay of the NRA. Recently, local communities have begun to enact Living Wage laws, which apply to local government employees and which set an effective example for other employers. They serve to resist at least somewhat the growing gap between the rich and the poor in that particular community. At the time of this writing, local communities are constructing and instituting "fairness ordinances," which, in the absence of state and federal laws, provide for treating people fairly in employment and housing, for example, regardless of their sexual orientation or gender identity.[2]

Resistance serves to restore a covenantal understanding of political processes. It "links humans together" for a "mutual sharing of whatever things are useful and necessary for harmony."[3] Local congregations may not, by themselves, be expressions of the beloved community as we have defined it; but the religious community may contribute its own embedded unity (see chapter 1). To the extent that congregations are aware of and affirm their embedded relationships, they set an example and contribute to the unity of the body politic. Just affirming, tending to, and acting upon the embedded unity of the faith community locally is potentially an act of resistance. Dominant communities are not necessarily edified by local religious unity; nor are those of the religious community who seek a position of power within the dominant community (see p. 86 above). But the local community of faith, when it acts on the basis of embedded unity, may, if it so chooses, nudge the local body politic into itself becoming an entity of resistance, partly because covenant informed language and political understanding continue to have some currency.[4]

The Beloved Community — Resistance and Hope

Beloved ... it does not yet appear what we shall be....
— 1 John 3:2

In 1993, just when people of Grand Rapids, Michigan, had thought they had surmounted racism and had "been there and done that"; just when they were ready to move on to other, more easily solvable problems, a community ministry in the city proposed a community-wide antiracism emphasis — an Institute for Racial Justice. While no particular crisis prompted it, the ministry perceived that it was time to acknowledge that racism persisted in the community and that the ministry could not responsibly continue to deny this reality. This conclusion forced itself upon the ministry as it gradually became aware that disparate segments of the community — from churches to nonprofit organizations to retail and other businesses — were once more placing concerns about racism on their agenda. As yet there is no evidence that the actual racial/ethnic relations in the community have improved, but the ministry nevertheless continues to address the issue in a variety of ways.[5]

This ongoing and seemingly fruitless struggle against racism will find an echo in many local ecumenical and interfaith community ministries. Yet a covenant hope perdures. In 1995, the ecumenical Faith in the City Forum of the city of Bradford, England (where race riots had recently occurred), published a report called "Powerful Whispers." It focused on four neighborhoods where hearings were conducted to determine what the main concerns and issues were in each of these communities. These neighborhoods were referred to as "Urban Priority Areas" — that is, they were high on the government's Index of Urban Deprivation. The report emphasized the interrelation between these neighborhoods and the Bradford metropolitan area as a whole:

> We believe that God created heaven and earth, and that God has infinite love and concern for every part of creation, beyond anything that we can imagine. . . . We believe that the inspiration, motivation and energy that comes from the Spirit of God can be discovered in certain kinds of places: where people come together to build a better community — when there is much to drive them apart; where people contribute and receive as equals — when in many ways they are not equal; where people discover new horizons and concerns — when it is safer simply to look after self and family; where people give each other hope — when there is plenty to feel hopeless about.[6]

This report illustrates how the burden of community ministry is to mediate hope in the local community at large. Insofar as this hope is acted upon, the political processes and diverse people that compose a beloved community come into play.[7]

One way to epitomize these processes is to say with Althusius that we may hope and strive for a mutual sharing of whatever things are necessary and useful for harmony and productive activity in social life. I submit that a covenant construct of triadic relationships, in which a people in all their diversity pledge their trust to one another in devotion to a higher power or cause, is the best model that can be had for local political life. "Best" because it may bring hope, fairness, and unity to local communities, which, although under siege, are our best hope for a restoration of covenantal responsibility. In propagating the style and language of covenant, ecumenical and interfaith community ministry may make a singular contribution. Covenanted community entails "making the conditions of others your own" (Winthrop; see above p. 18). Covenanted community is deeply relational, making hopelessness, however justified by appearances, not an option. Sharon Welch writes, "I am pulled back from self-indulgent ennui and despair only as I remain in community with those who are oppressed and are struggling against that oppression."[8] Authentic community ministry places the plight of the poor and oppressed into the line of vision of its middle-class constituency in the knowledge of our interrelatedness and of a future that depends on the participation of all in the cause of sustainable community.[9]

Here we might well borrow the word "solidarity" from liberationists. Community ministry may bring hope to the entire local community by encouraging solidarity among the oppressed, proposing actions in solidarity with them, and by thus being proactive in the face of global forces that are oppressive of people, destructive of Earth, and inimical to sustainable communities. This solidarity is not an achievement of will or a presumption of knowing the reality of the other so much as it is an awareness that we humans are always already in the covenant as those who have always already broken the covenant.[10]

To bring hope into local communities is a high calling. The churches of a community forfeit this privilege unless they first demonstrate their own embedded unity, and in so doing resist local and supra-local domination systems.[11] Each interfaith and ecumenical community ministry will claim this right of resistance if it is to have any integrity vis-à-vis the dominant community, which uses the divisions in the religious community to further its own purposes. In so doing, community ministry becomes a channel of the hope that defines the beloved community.[12] This process begins but does not end in understanding the theological importance of the ecumenical and interfaith relationships upon which community ministry depends. Out of these very relationships may come a significant contribution to the sustainability of the local community.

Resistance and hope are companion themes of the process that is the beloved community. Memories of hope prompt resistance, and resistance makes more memories of hope. Sharon Welch speaks of the paucity, frailty, and rarity of resistance but also of the memories of actual resistance leading to liberation that keeps the spirit of resistance alive.[13] Many are memories of liberation among African Americans, women, and the poor — memories that community ministry may draw upon insofar as it embraces, respects, and includes those who treasure them. These memories are both the fruits and the seeds of authentic resistance within the dominant community. They are the stuff of hope in our local communities. This is why, in the light of recurrent racism, African American liberation represents one of the key memories and agendas of authentic community ministry.[14]

When the ecumenical coalition of Bradford made its report in 1995, it could not have imagined that in spite of all their efforts to build "solidarity and community" (their words), six years later there would be urban uprisings in the vicinity the likes of which Bradford had never seen. Certainly if any community had taken precautions, this was the one. Therefore, if any community now had cause to feel demoralized and hopeless it was this one. What the Bradford experience and the experience of so many other community ministries teach us, especially in regard to racism, is that where Christianity and other religions fail is at the level of practice in the local community. When we fail, it is not so much a question of hoping for too much as it is of hoping for too little — in light of the memories of liberation uncovered in our collective and individual histories.

So, in Bradford, hope was not extinguished by a summer's violence in the streets. Instead the community of hope expanded from an ecumenical to an interfaith entity. A group called Interfaith Women For Peace was formed some ten years ago. In 1995 it was instrumental in halting riots when its members walked into the scene carrying placards calling for peace. The group met regularly to pray for peace. When disturbances again broke out in the summer of 2001 and when, on September 11, 2001, militant Muslim fundamentalists attacked the United States, the relevance and activity of the group grew to the point that now it is a major focus of ecumenical efforts in Bradford.

Thus an extravagant but authenticated hope lives in the beloved community. This hope leads to what Gutiérrez called "a conversion to the neighbor, the oppressed person, the exploited class, the despised race, the dominated country."[15] This hope is a concrete political hope — a *covenantal* hope. It must be local in the sense that it must be translated into local politics in order to be fully realized. Any local community might claim this hope and experience of the beloved community.[16]

Housing as a Stage-Set for the Appearance of the Beloved Community

My ancestors came from the Netherlands to settle Holland, Michigan, in the 1840s, and their leader was a Calvinist minister. Did they view this task in the light of a covenantal standard? The oral history of the community emphasizes the bone-breaking task of digging out by hand the enormous tree stumps. Did these determined people reflect upon their incursion into the primeval forest? Did they give thought to how their building of houses might also build their sense of community? Was there a pooling of resources so that the poorest among them received adequate shelter? Did their number include those with special housing needs, and were they met? Were there wide disparities in the economic value of land parcels, and were steps taken to prevent unfairness in real estate transactions? What was the tenor of their relations with Indians and English-born trapper/merchants who preceded them to this place as they cleared the land and built their houses? The answers to these questions would provide quite a comprehensive account of the beginnings of this settlement.

In today's Holland, Michigan, one finds numerous churches of various Calvinist persuasions and a broad representation of other denominations. Do these congregations have any sense of their embedded unity and the effect that it might have on the town's continuing development? As the building of houses continues apace, what is its impact on Lake Michigan, a part of the largest freshwater system in the world — a system that may be on the brink of an ecological disaster? With Mexican Americans (who formerly were itinerant workers in the surrounding orchards) now purchasing most of the housing in the residential core of the city, what is the quality of the relations between them and their congregations and the majority Dutch American population? We see that all of the questions we posed about the settlement of the town may be asked about today's community with slight variations, and that the answers to these and other questions related to housing would provide a fairly complete picture of the community 150-plus years after its founding.

Cases in Point

• One community ministry allied itself with the national Interfaith Hospitality Network to provide training and other resources to congregations so that they could respond to growing numbers of homeless families. Congregations alternate in providing overnight lodging and meals in their facilities. A paid director with the help of large numbers of volunteers from congregations coordinates and staffs the program on an interfaith basis. The Network's literature invokes the passages from Leviticus that we have cited above as well as Deuteronomy 24:17–22, which implores the hearers to leave a portion of the harvest for the stranger and asking them to remember that they themselves once were strangers [slaves] in a strange land. They also cite one of the most compelling passages in Hebrew scripture on the unity of humankind — Isaiah 58:7: "Is not this the fast that I choose: to loose the bonds of injustice, to undo the thongs of the yoke, to let the oppressed go free, and to break every yoke? Is it not to share your bread with the hungry, and bring the homeless poor into your house; when you see the naked to cover them, and not to hide yourself from your own (human) flesh?"

The Interfaith Hospitality Network embraces the thesis of this book when it speaks of "a universal principle declared in Leviticus and embodied in Jesus' words and works, 'Love thy neighbor as thyself.' When we follow this commandment with practical, tangible actions, we unlock and follow the deepest, most spiritual impulses of our human hearts."[17]

• Another community ministry took advantage of a federal housing program to build affordable housing for elderly, disabled, and handicapped persons. This ministry discovered that it had the highest percentage of elderly persons in its county and that, because of rising rents and housing costs, these longtime residents were being forced to move, against their will, away from the neighborhood, the shops and services and neighbors that were so important in their daily life. This is clearly an example of a community ministry entering the field of housing out of a sense of pastoral care for the community. This housing project illustrates our point that the beloved community is a kind of amalgam that links the religious and local civil community in processes that makes the latter a better place in which to live.

• It would be hard to find an issue that more clearly separates the sheep from the goats in connection with our argument than the NIMBY (Not In My Back Yard) syndrome. In almost every local community there are individuals who are prepared to exclude those who have special housing needs because of age, income, and disability. But this reality is only illustrative of our contention that the true battleground in the struggle to resist the domination system is the local community and its daily life. In Massachusetts, for example, where there is a state-mandated goal that every community make 10 percent of its housing supply accessible to moderate-income families, only 24 out of 361 communities comply. Plymouth, Minnesota, a suburb of Minneapolis, has adopted a comprehensive plan with a provision that 20 percent of new rental and other housing must be affordable to low-and moderate-income persons. This action was taken mainly because of the encouragement and educational efforts of the Metropolitan Interfaith Council on Affordable Housing (MICAH), which now seeks to use the Plymouth model in conversations with other wealthy Minneapolis suburbs. The plan specifically enjoins developers to include housing for moderate- and low-income employees and residents in the community and provides for a review process to enforce the rule. MICAH claims that in the past three years, local congregations have won approval for more than seven hundred low-income housing units, prevented the demolition of more than seventeen hundred structurally sound such units in which primarily racial, ethnic minorities resided, and influenced the stated housing plans of fourteen communities. An important resource for MICAH and other coalitions of congregations that are addressing this issue is the monthly NIMBY report of the National Low Income Housing Coalition (NLIHC). It relates successes and setbacks as it seeks to promote inclusive communities.

• A community ministry formed a community development corporation (CDC) for the specific purpose of developing low- and moderate-income housing on the affluent side of town. While the assumption had been that high costs would prevent such housing from being constructed, this nonprofit development corporation has been able to build several dozen houses over a five-year period by taking advantage of various government and private programs that reduce the costs of land, loans, and construction. The rationale for this program is the one often used for "scattered-site housing" — low-income housing that is scattered throughout a community rather than concentrated in a particular neighborhood. This approach resists the strictly market-based forces that would result in segregation by class, making poor neighborhoods still poorer, reducing the quality of public and private services to those neighborhoods, making them politically less powerful and vulnerable to a host of injustices, including the practices of "redlining" by banks or toxic dumping by corporations. In a word, scattered-site housing counters the ghettoizing and stigmatization of low-income families and individuals. It makes it more likely that such families will become fully participating and politically empowered citizens.[18]

• In a small-city neighborhood in southern Indiana, a denomination had to abandon a large building that had once been used as a hospital and then as a retirement home. It was a landmark, the largest building in the area and, of course, the building to which many residents pointed as the place of their birth. Because of the presence of asbestos in the otherwise structurally sound building, a buyer was hard to find. The community ministry there successfully pushed for the formation of a CDC for the express purpose of finding redevelopment solutions for the future of the building. With the community ministry playing an active part in the work of the CDC, the building is soon to become an apartment house for low- and moderate-income families. This is an illustration of the impact of housing decisions on planning, land use, and environmental factors.

• In the Tenderloin district of San Francisco, a community ministry, using governmental, church, and other private sources of funding, sponsored a housing project designed to meet the needs of street people and other numerous poor of that area. Without previous experience in the housing field, the San Francisco Network Ministries, led by its director of twenty-two years, Glenda Hope, a Presbyterian minister, developed the 555 Ellis Street Family Apartments. The "Affordable Housing Design Advisor" calls this project "part of an ongoing effort by local nonprofit organizations to provide family housing in a neighborhood with few multiple-bedroom units and to reverse the long-standing negative image of the Tenderloin." This project is also a pastoral response to a whole neighborhood, and it takes on the additional burden of attempting to influence the overall character of the community so that it is more hospitable to families. Many community meetings produced suggestions that molded the project. Among the suggestions that were accepted was one that led to designing storefronts as lighted cases to display artworks of residents of the Tenderloin on a rotating basis. Also included are a large community recreation room, a garden, a patio, a courtyard, a resource library, and a tutorial center with computer stations. The building houses very low- and low-income families in thirty-nine units ranging from three studios to nineteen three-bedroom apartments. The striking aspect of this project, however, is a uniqueness derived from the uniqueness of the local community. In fact, the women's organization source, which leveraged most of the funding, stresses the criteria of local self-determination and coalition building. These are, at root, theological criteria that do encourage and support community ministry. As it stands, the building is an illustration of how a ministry takes its cue from its own community and bends national and regional resources to suit its community rather than the reverse.

San Francisco Network Ministries states on its Web site (www.sfnetworkministries.org) that it

> is devoted to the people of the Tenderloin neighborhood... with whom we work cooperatively for the empowerment of all, proclaiming good news for the poor and seeking liberty for those who are oppressed... We are like the "woman who took a measure of leaven and hid it in the dough." We draw together coalitions to work on particular concerns and we enter into existing coalitions.... We engage in political organizing, advocacy and direct action for systemic change.... We are like those lighting a lamp and setting it on a stand so that it may give light to all and glory to God. We believe that everyone has been given gifts for the common good, and we seek to draw out and affirm those gifts through personal, face-to-face ministry.

The 555 Ellis Street project is an illustration of how important the housing field might be for such covenantal statements, which emphasize "systemic change" in the interface between the religious and civil communities.

• One of the first community ministries established a fair housing center as one of its first projects — Suffolk Housing Services (SHS) in Suffolk County (Long Island), New York. SHS began as just a listing of rental properties but eventually became one of the largest fair housing litigation centers in the United States. In cooperation with the National Committee Against Discrimination in Housing, it broke legal ground through landmark cases in the field in the 1970s. SHS sought to break the segregated pattern of rapid suburbanization that had been occurring in the township of Brookhaven and in so doing affected that pattern over a much wider area.

Repairing the Broken Covenant (V)

The field of housing is where we find the most problematic use of covenant. It is hard now to imagine how important the issue of fair housing was in the United States in the 1960s and 1970s. In fact it was the headline issue just before the Vietnam War took center stage; the entire civil rights movement tended to devolve upon it. It was (and to some extent still is) a struggle of major determinative influence upon American culture, and it was a local struggle above all in which the word "covenant" played an important role. It was not uncommon to encounter explicitly exclusive "covenants" by which entire communities, neighborhoods, and subdivisions attempted to exclude whole classes of people and even to make illegal their presence as residents. Today these "covenants" are implicit in the buying and selling arrangements of private, gated communities throughout the United States.

On the other hand, one of the main ways that people of faith demonstrated their resistance to the regnant patterns of residential segregation in the 1960s was to sign "open housing covenants." These campaigns were used to influence local government policies and individual buyers and sellers as well as ecclesiastical politics. Many local churches officially supported such covenants.

Are both uses of "covenant" equally valid in this struggle? Not if we seek to respond to the summary of biblical law that is crucial to a covenantal understanding of community: "You shall love the Holy One, your God, with all your heart, and with all your soul, and with all your mind," and

"You shall love your neighbor as yourself" (Matt. 22:36–
40; Deut. 6:5; Lev. 19:18; Matt. 19:19; see also Lev. 19:34:
"You must love the stranger as yourself." An exclusionary
housing covenant is a contradiction in terms.[19]

This covenant way of thinking is a gift to the entire
community, its creatures, and its natural environment. It
would be opposed to exclusionary housing patterns that pre-
supposed a dominant class. Exclusionary communities are
essentially defensive arrangements based on the antitheses
of resistance and hope — accommodation and fear. Engaging locally in the field of housing may be an effective means
of restoring covenant thinking to the community.

Conclusion

I have tried to show that the web of relationships that covenant implies has a great deal of relevance for local interfaith and ecumenical community ministry. As informed by both biblical exegesis and its function in American political history, covenant assumes local community as a primary theological referent. As such it has potential as a counterbalance against the forces of globalism and regionalization. It lends theological weight to any advocacy on behalf of "sustainable community" (Rasmussen) as opposed to "sustainable development." It responds to a challenge that is relevant to community ministry: how can we begin to form redeemed communities that are characterized by both justice and nonviolence (Albrecht)?

Local community is revelatory — that is, it provides clues for ethical action on a collective or communal basis that may be discerned at first only on a local scale.

As community ministry searches out these clues and responds to them, it may acquire a countercultural identity, especially where interfaith relations come into play, and where affirming an embedded unity among congregations contradicts the competitive values of society at large. This combination of covenant relationships and local interreligious unity, while promoting sustainable community, also produces a brew that is inherently subversive of large systems of domination that threaten local community.

A principle of inclusivity and a principle of resistance are both central to an understanding of covenant — embracing the entire body politic on a local scale and opposing domination systems in which our lives are enmeshed. Embedded unity, then, may have a transforming effect on local community. Greater empowerment of the rank and file of church membership along with interfaith-based citizenship training proceeds from a covenant principle of inclusivity. Greater efforts to eliminate racism and to negotiate effective cooperation between predominantly African American and predominantly European American congregations spring from a principle of resistance, countering racist practices in the immediate societal context.

The potential of embedded religious unity has not gone unnoticed, and there are those who would exploit it for causes that, however admirable in themselves, may not place the interests of local community foremost. Authentic ecumenical and interfaith community ministry views embedded unity as an engine that protects the integrity of local community as a matter of divine mandate.

Even and especially as it promulgates inclusion and resistance, authentic community ministry takes its cue from the local community. It partakes of the uniqueness of the community that it serves while being driven by the embedded unity of its congregations.

Notes

Introduction

1. Eric Mount, *Covenant, Community and Common Good* (Cleveland: Pilgrim, 1999).

2. Norbert Lohfink and Erich Zenger, *The God of Israel and the Nations* (Collegeville, Minn.: Liturgical Press, 2000).

3. Ibid., 192.

4. Mount, *Covenant, Community and Common Good,* 26.

5. Daniel Judah Elazar, *The Covenant Tradition in Politics,* 4 vols. (New Brunswick, N.J.: Transaction Publishers, 1995–98).

1. The Congregations

1. Gary Gunderson, *Deeply Woven Roots* (Minneapolis: Fortress, 1997).

2. George W. Webber, *The Congregation in Mission* (New York: Abingdon, 1964), 12.

3. Ibid., 192.

4. Ibid., 89–90.

5. See, for example, the archives of the First Presbyterian Church of Rochester, New York — now part of a merged congregation, the Downtown United Presbyterian Church — where, in about 1895, a rabbi, along with other non-Presbyterian religious leaders, participated in the celebration of the seventy-fifth anniversary of the founding of the congregation.

6. James F. Hopewell, *Congregation: Stories and Structures,* ed. Barbara G. Wheeler (Philadelphia: Fortress, 1987).

7. The fact that it is left for us to add that last parenthetical phrase indicates a remarkable flaw in the congregational studies movement — namely, that it does not treat of relationships between congregations, much less study the texture and meaning of those relationships. From the beginning of the movement, each congregation has been seen as an entity unto itself in respect to the surrounding faith communities. We may

view this oversight in sharp relief in an otherwise admirably thorough work, which is an analysis of the congregation in its social context: Nancy Ammerman, *Congregation and Community* (New Brunswick, N.J.: Rutgers University Press, 1997). Except for noting near the end of the book that congregations have the capacity to make various connections, including those with neighboring congregations, the book is a paean to the particularism of congregational life in the United States. Moreover (and this reflects a second flaw in the congregational studies movement), the book is an uncritical analysis, inviting a rather romantic perception overall. As to particularism: although as noted above, it may be seen as a positive factor in the development of relations among congregations, one notes a bias in congregational studies research against any hint of universalism that would allow the author to spy out the deeply embedded relationships between people of faith in any given community. As to the lack of critical perspective, it derives from the intention of congregational studies to be "corrective," that is, to provide a counterweight to the considerable criticism that was directed at the congregation during the 1960s and after. See James P. Wind and James W. Lewis, *American Congregations* (Chicago: University of Chicago Press, 1994), 2:4–10.

8. Dietrich Bonhoeffer, *Life Together* (New York: Harper, 1954), 26.

9. Ibid., 37–38.

10. Elizabeth O'Connor, *The New Community* (New York: Harper & Row, 1976), 3.

11. Ibid., 96.

12. Ibid., 58.

13. Robert Bellah, *The Broken Covenant: American Civil Religion in a Time of Trial* (New York: Seabury, 1975).

14. This famous sermon entitled "A Modell of Christian Charity" may be found in its entirety in Perry Miller and Thomas H. Johnson, *The Puritans* (New York: American Book Co., 1938), 195–99.

15. When asked what is the greatest commandment, Jesus gave two. He said, " 'You shall love the Lord your God with all your heart, and with all your soul, and with all your mind.' This is the greatest and first commandment. And a second is like it: 'You shall love your neighbor as yourself. On these two commandments depend all the law and the prophets' " (Matt. 22:37–39). This "second" one originates in Leviticus 19:18 ("You shall love your neighbor as yourself"), while the first half of Jesus' summary of the law will be found in Deuteronomy 6:5 ("And you shall love the Holy One, your God with all your heart, and with all your soul, and with all your might)." Paul, writing to the Romans, says that all the commandments are summed up in this sentence, "You shall love your neighbor as yourself" (13:9); and "One who loves one's neighbor has fulfilled the law" (13:8); and again in the letter to the Galatians: "For the whole law is fulfilled in one word, 'You shall love your neighbor as yourself' " (5:14). Also in the letter of James we find, "If you really fulfill

the royal law according to the scripture, 'You shall love your neighbor as yourself,' you do well" (2:8).

16. Bellah, *The Broken Covenant*, xi.

17. Ibid., xii–xiii.

18. Ibid., 141–42.

19. Clinton E. Gardner, *The Church as a Prophetic Community* (Philadelphia: Westminster, 1967), 231.

20. See "Renewing the Welfare Covenant," in *Living Responsibly in Community*, ed. Frederick E. Glennon, Gary S. Hauk, and Darryl M. Trimiew (Lanham, Md.: University Press of America, 1997).

21. Glennon speaks of "the real promise of the Judeo-Christian tradition of covenant for our pluralistic society," namely, "that we are social beings who have a bondedness that transcends our individual self-interests. By stressing the need for mutual respect and mutual responsibility and the need for common, disinterested deliberation about the direction and goals of our society, a covenantal perspective opens the door for more substantive solutions to the problem of poverty than we have had in the past." With Glennon, I opt for the broadest and most inclusive use of the term "covenant," for which I believe there is strong biblical warrant: "(1) Covenants are inclusive of all members of the community; (2) The covenant stresses mutual obligation and responsibility; (3) The covenant has a vision of community designed to produce a society that encourages the meaningful participation and well-being of all; (4) Covenant community is egalitarian; (5) The covenant community has a special concern for the poor and marginalized; (6) The covenant deals with internal dispositions as well as external actions" (ibid., 179).

22. Rosetta E. Ross, "A Womanist Model of Responsibility: The Moral Agency of Victoria Way DeLee," in *Living Responsibly in Community*, ed. Frederick E. Glennon, Gary S. Hauk, and Darryl M. Trimiew (Lanham, Md.: University Press of America, 1997), 91.

23. Ibid., 107.

24. Peter Paris, *The Spirituality of African Peoples* (Minneapolis: Fortress, 1995), 86.

25. C. Eric Lincoln and Lawrence H. Mamiya, *The Black Church in the African American Experience* (Durham, N.C.: Duke University Press, 1990), 5.

26. Ibid., 73.

27. Mary R. Sawyer, *Black Ecumenism* (Valley Forge, Pa.: Trinity Press International, 1994), 8.

28. Ibid., 112.

29. Robert Wuthnow, *Acts of Compassion* (Princeton, N.J.: Princeton University Press, 1991).

30. Ibid., 269–70.

31. Ibid., 280.

32. Ibid., 300.

33. George Peck and John S. Hofman, eds., *The Laity in Ministry* (Valley Forge, Pa.: Judson, 1984).

34. Excellent examples may be found in James A. Adams and Celia Hahn, *Learning to Share the Ministry* (Washington, D.C.: Alban Institute, 1975); Cameron Hall: *Lay Action: The Church's Third Force* (New York: Friendship Press, 1974); Hendrik Kraemer, *A Theology of the Laity* (Philadelphia: Westminster, 1958). Kraemer points to a key text for the theology of the laity: "All Christians are truly priests and there is no distinction amongst them except as to office... Everybody who is baptized may maintain that he has been consecrated as priest, bishop or pope" (Martin Luther, "To the Christian Nobility" [Kraemer, 61]). Kraemer noted that the word "laity" is from the Greek *laos*, meaning people, and he stressed that in one sense the laity is the church — the people of God. As such, the "people" are one of the three major terms in the basic covenant that God has established (the other two being Godself and humanity/creation at large): "The word 'laos' is, in the sense of people of God, applied to Israel in order to express God's special relation to this people.... This relation to God rests on a divine covenant, a divine act of election" (Kraemer, *A Theology of the Laity*, 155–57).

35. In Peck and Hofman, eds., *The Laity in Ministry*, 21.

2. The Local Body Politic and Community Ministry

1. In order to interpret the social location of ecumenical urban ministry, Webber turned to the word "politics": "I suggest that politics serve as the perspective from which to examine our theological consensus on the mission of the congregation" (George W. Webber, *The Congregation in Mission* [New York: Abingdon, 1964], 49). I agree that politics serves as a perspective — a covenantal perspective — from which to interpret the mission of the congregation. By politics I mean the political/economic/cultural processes that shape and determine the character of the local body politic.

2. Elizabeth O'Connor, *The New Community* (New York: Harper & Row, 1976), 58. Johanna Bos says: "Justice is a key word for a proper understanding of the nature of God's relation to the creation and specifically to the covenant community. Rather than understanding love and justice in tension with each other, the Bible depicts God's justice as inseparable from God's love. More precisely, God's justice is the expression of God's particular concern for categories of people that are by definition the most vulnerable ones in a given community.... The listing of orphan, widow, and stranger in Deuteronomy 10 (Dt. 10:17–18) is not an isolated instance, nor is the list coincidental. Widow, orphan and stranger constitute together throughout the Hebrew Bible a category of people who exist by definition on the margin of life. They are people who in the social reality of ancient Israel are deprived from a context that gives them automatically a measure of security. In the Torah these are the people for

whom special care and protection is demanded because when they cry out to God, God hears their cry (cf. Exod. 22:23).... That justice is closely related to God's steadfast love is expressed clearly in Jeremiah 9:24: 'Let those who boast boast in this, that they understand and know me, that I am the Lord; I act with steadfast love, justice, and righteousness in the earth, for in these things I delight; says the Lord.' *Here the context for the execution of justice is wider than that of the covenant community alone. God's concern is ultimately for the whole creation and for those who suffer injustice from the hands of their neighbor in all of created existence"* (Johanna W. H. van Wijk-Bos, "Solidarity with the Stranger," in *A Journey to Justice* [Louisville: Presbyterian Committee on the Self-Development of Peoples, Presbyterian Church (USA), 1993], 46–47; emphasis added).

3. Brueggemann says: "[Ancient Israel's] primal speech of covenanting concerns governance, sovereignty, public order, public policy, public possibility and the sanctions that go with such social transactions. Thus the dominant metaphor of Israel's faith is from the outset public and not narrowly Israelite." Walter Brueggemann, *Interpretation and Obedience* (Minneapolis: Fortress, 1991), 71. Interestingly enough, the same dynamic marked the revival of the language of covenanting in the sixteenth century. First came Althusius, who, although he borrowed the concept from scripture, used it to describe political relationships. Only later did the Swiss reformer Heinrich Bullinger put the term at the center of his theology.

4. Webber, *The Congregation in Mission*, 89–90.

5. James Cone, "Black Ecumenism and the Liberation Struggle" (Lecture, Louisville Presbyterian Theological Seminary, Audio Cassette #1396). Likewise, the theologian Juan Luis Segundo says that to attempt to disconnect theology from politics means to engage in either self-delusion or deception: "Every theology is political, even one that does not speak or think in political terms. The influence of politics on theology and every other cultural sphere cannot be evaded any more than the influence of theology on politics and other forms of human thinking. The worst politics of all [and the worst theology of all? — ADB] would be to let theology perform this function unconsciously, for that brand of politics is always bound up with the status quo" (Juan Luis Segundo, *The Liberation of Theology* [Maryknoll, N.Y.: Orbis Books, 1976], 74–75).

6. "Indeed Jesus seems to go so far as to suggest that one cannot recognize Christ, and therefore come to know God, unless he or she is willing to start with a personal commitment to the oppressed" (Segundo, *Liberation of Theology*, 81).

7. Sharon Welch, *Communities of Resistance and Solidarity* (Maryknoll, N.Y.: Orbis Books, 1985), 74.

8. Ibid., 77.

9. Emil Fackenheim, *To Mend the World* (New York: Schocken Books, 1984), 256.

10. Gloria Albrecht, *The Character of Our Communities: Toward an Ethic of Liberation for the Church* (Nashville: Abingdon, 1995), 139.

11. Ibid., 142. Words in brackets are mine.

12. This is the central thesis of Juan Luis Segundo in his book *the Liberation of Theology* Maryknoll, N.Y.: Orbis Books, 1976).

13. About this danger, Albrecht comments: "There can be no unproblematic appropriation of our tradition, our scriptures and our stories. We approach them as people located in a particular Christian community that gives us a way of interpreting these texts. When our location is in a community of privilege (whether by race, class, ethnicity, gender, or sexual orientation), we are in danger of missing the history of struggle and resistance to social privilege that is the history of our faith" (Albrecht, *Character of Our Communities*, 152).

14. Ibid., 159.

15. "Knowledges 'from below' break in and reveal the violence in middle class peace. Diversity, understood as the empowerment of disqualified knowledges, is necessary to truth and goodness. It is an epistemological and moral necessity. The dilemma that those of us who inhabit the dominant culture face is how to place ourselves where we will be confronted by the reality of others. I am not referring to the reality of those who have been stripped bare by injustices and whose immediate survival needs solicit our charity. Such encounters often serve only to secure us in our dominance. Too often, in the soup kitchens that are increasingly essential to the physical lives of some city residents, we who are dominant feed our sense of innocence and powerlessness. I am referring instead to our response to the invitation extended by bell hooks, the invitation to enter that space of creativity and power in the margins, to enter the sites of resistance — resistance to our innocence and the social power that protects it" (Welch, *Communities of Resistance and Solidarity*, 159).

16. Albrecht, *Character of Our Communities*, 164.

17. Marvin Ellison, "Holding Up Our Half of the Sky: Male Gender Privilege as Problem and Resource for Liberation Ethics," *Journal of Feminist Studies in Religion* 9, nos. 1 and 2 (1993): 95–113.

18. Albrecht, *Character of Our Communities*, 167.

19. Ibid., 166–67.

20. Ibid., 167.

21. Martin Buber, *I and Thou* (Edinburgh: T. & T. Clark, 1937), 120.

22. "But one's relation to the 'special something' that usurps the throne of the supreme value of one's life, and supplants eternity, rests always on experiencing and using an It, a thing, an object of enjoyment. For this relation alone is able to obstruct the prospect which opens toward God — it is the impenetrable world of It; but the relation which involves the saying of the Thou opens up this prospect ever anew. One who is dominated by the idol that one wishes to win, to hold, and to

keep — possessed by a desire of possession — has no way to God but that of reversal, which is a change not only of goal but also of the nature of one's movement. The one who is possessed is saved by being wakened and educated to solidarity of relation. . . . The bright building of community, to which there is an escape, even from the dungeon of 'social life,' is the achievement of the same power that works in relation between humanity and God. This does not mean that the one relation is set beside the others; for it is the universal relation, into which all streams pour, yet without exhausting their waters. Who wishes to make division and define boundaries between sea and streams? There we find only the one flow from I to Thou, unending, the one boundless flow of the real life" (ibid., 105, 107).

Another thinker who depends on the thought of Buber is Emmanuel Lévinas. See his article "Dialogue: Self-Consciousness and Proximity of the Neighbor," in *Of God Who Comes to Mind,* trans. Bettina Bergo (Stanford, Calif.: Stanford University Press, 1998). (This article, in my opinion, would be a good starting point for anyone who wanted to develop a philosophy of community ministry.) "Dialogue is the non-indifference of the you to the I — a chance for what we must — perhaps with prudence — call love. . . . It is in the dialogue of transcendence that the idea of the good arises, merely by the fact itself that, in the encounter, the other counts above all else. . . . The concreteness of the good is the worth of the other person. . . . Dialogue is thus not merely a way of speaking. . . . It is transcendence. . . . Better again . . . transcendence has no meaning except by way of an I saying You. . . . That a human spirituality might be possible which does not begin in knowledge, or in the psyche as experience, and that the relation to the you in its purity be the relation to the invisible God is, no doubt, a new view on the human psyche. . . . Yet this is also important for the orientation of theology: the God of prayer, of invocation, would be more ancient than the God deduced from the world. . . . The old biblical theme of humanity made in the image of God takes on a new meaning, but it is in the 'you' and not in the 'I' that this resemblance is announced. The very moment that leads to another leads to God" (147–48).

23. William E. May, *Becoming Human* (Canton, Ohio: Pflaum Publishing, 1975), 133–34.

24. The following quotation captures some of the irreducible aspects of the local from an existential perspective: "No longer do the false hopes of democracy/revolution/development/consumption let me off the hook. I am really Here and it doesn't go away. I cannot dream it away/sleep it away/cry it away/smoke it away/drink it away/eat it away/buy it away/love it away. . . . I do not know why Here was made this way but so long as I live Here, to be truly alive, I have to accept and acknowledge all of this pain and despair that makes Here Here. Here is where I must confront the reality of my being and all that which would deny me the awareness

of the task or the means to accomplish it" (Bill Smith in *Liberation Ideologies, Postmodernism and the Americas,* ed. David Batstone [London: Routledge, 1997], 167).

25. Sharon Welch, *A Feminist Ethic of Risk* (Minneapolis: Fortress, 1990), 20.

26. Josiah Royce, *The Problem of Christianity* (Chicago: University of Chicago Press, 1968 [1918]).

27. Ibid., 85.

28. Ibid., 84.

3. Community Ministry in Theological/Historical Context— An Excursion

1. See my article "Community Ministry: The Wild Card in Ecumenical Relations and Social Ministry," *Journal of Ecumenical Studies* 25, no. 4 (Fall 1988).

2. From the standpoint of community ministry it is an article of faith that the local community, defined as a social-political-theological entity, may be a true meeting place for various cultures and that a theology of this meeting place would indeed transcend cultural differences. Seen in this light, the works of Robert J. Schreiter are problematic for community ministry because Schreiter defines the local in terms of culture. Thus, his "local" is not our "local" but is, in fact, a trans-local phenomenon. I submit that Schreiter's concern is to construct particular, culture-specific theologies rather than local ones. Because he does not actually allow for local differences within particular cultures, the practical upshot of this theory would be akin to an apartheid approach — sanctioning culture-based theologies that would disguise the embedded unity that I have posited. See especially Schreiter, *Constructing Local Theologies* (Maryknoll, N.Y.: Orbis Books, 1985), 20–21. See also *The New Catholicity* (Maryknoll, N.Y.: Orbis Books, 1997), 73, where Schreiter defines resistance on behalf of the local in strictly cultural terms.

3. See the author's "Redefining the Ecumenical Movement," in *A Practical Guide to Community Ministry* (Louisville: Westminster/John Knox, 1993), 31–43.

4. David A. Bos, "The Establishment of Ecumenical Local Mission in North American Church Life," *Journal of Ecumenical Studies* 22, no. 1 (Winter 1985).

5. An excellent contemporary overview of this period of experimentation may be found in Rudiger Reitz, *The Church in Experiment* (Nashville: Abingdon, 1969).

6. Colin Williams, *Where in the World* (New York: National Council of Churches, 1963), and *What in the World* (New York: National Council of Churches, 1964); Steve Rose, *The Grass Roots Church* (New York: Holt, Rinehart and Winston, 1966).

7. "There is then a strong case for rejecting the conclusion that the residential congregation is necessarily the normal form of church life. It seems possible that the deep attachment to this view is holding the church back from the freedom it needs to be re-formed in such a way that the presence of Christ can inform the secular patterns of everyday life" (Williams, *Where in the World*, 11).

8. "The Church that takes abandonment seriously will place emphasis on experimental ministries, on participation in direct action movements designed to bring about political, economic and racial justice, and on the mission of the laity in the scientific laboratories, the legislative assemblies, the centers of youth culture, the schools and the wretched compartments where the aged are prematurely buried" (Rose, *The Grass Roots Church*, 74).

9. In a private conversation with the author in the early 1970s, Hans Hoekendijk insisted that one should never speak of the church as having a mission — "The church is mission." In his opinion, the church had no identity or theologically defined reality apart from emptying itself in the world. The implication was that the institutional bastion, the local congregation, had to give up its physical plant and other assets, and dispense itself throughout the community in the form of house churches and other experimental ministries.

10. Gustavo Gutiérrez, *A Theology of Liberation* (Maryknoll, N.Y.: Orbis Books, 1973).

11. Unpublished document: David A. Bos and T. Peter Ryan, "Proposal for An Ecumenical Ministry in the Marketplace," 1967.

12. Gutiérrez, *A Theology of Liberation*, 208.

13. Ibid., 194–95.

14. It is instructive to note that the military coup in Brazil was explicitly antiecumenical. Ecumenical commitments and activities were reason for imprisonment by the government or disciplinary action by the denominations, the leaders of which were often associated with the leaders of the coup. (Meanwhile in the United States, governmental intelligence agencies, themselves implicated in the Brazilian coup, were investigating ecumenical groups that opposed the Vietnam War or, several years later, that supported the Sanctuary Movement and its harboring of political refugees from Central America.)

The American scholar/activist Richard Shaull, who was forced to leave Brazil at the time of the coup, was instrumental in making the Brazilian experience relevant to North Americans. In a book he wrote jointly with Gustavo Gutiérrez in 1977, he took a patently North American concern — "self-realization" — and treated it in the mode of liberation theology: "Ultimately, self-realization today is a matter of becoming subjects of our own life and destiny.... Human emancipation now means the struggle to overcome all hierarchies, all patterns of domination and subordination, all that robs each person of the opportunity to take increasing power over his/her life and choose what he/she wants to become" (Richard Shaull and Gustavo Gutiérrez, *Liberation and Change* [Atlanta: John Knox, 1977], 135–36). In a later book, he reflected specifically on the base communities and their relevance for North Americans: "The reinvention of the church is as important for [middle-class people] at this moment as it is for the poor; we must find the equivalent of the Christian base communities in our own situation of struggle.... These communities emerged as the result of years of struggle on the part of a few people who had been captivated by a vision of what a church of the poor could be and kept working at the formation of such a community until a breakthrough occurred. An equivalent of these communities may emerge among us as small groups of those whose faith has led them into the struggle for justice for poor and marginal people come together in a similar way. As we discover how to create a new quality of life in community, while drawing on and living out our faith, we will also be engaged in the reinvention of the church and will demonstrate, once again, what it means to be an *ecclesia reformata semper reformanda*" (Richard Shaull, *The Reformation and Liberation Theology* [Louisville: Westminster/John Knox, 1991], 101).

15. Shaull, *The Reformation and Liberation Theology,* 130.

16. Gustavo Gutiérrez comments frequently in his writings on the importance of local faith communities and of the base community movement in particular for liberation theology. These communities make it possible for liberation theology to ground itself in the actual sufferings and lives of the poor. Liberation theologies are always a reflection on these grassroots communities. See the introduction to the revised edition of *A Theology of Liberation* (Maryknoll, N.Y.: Orbis Books, 1988), xix–xx.

17. By way of underlining this point, it is next to impossible, for example, for us honestly to follow the liberationist thinker Mark Taylor, whose social mission strategy has to do with developing countervailing forces against the TNCs. His "four strategic practices" to that end are all legitimate admonishments to community ministry, except that they are all to be used in the overarching goal of overcoming the power of the TNC. See "Transnational Corporations and Violence" in *New Visions for the Americas,* ed. David Batstone (Minneapolis: Fortress, 1993), 119–24. But community ministry is inextricably related to the power of TNCs!

18. Sharon Welch, "Dreams of the Good," in *New Visions for the Americas,* ed. David Batstone (Minneapolis: Fortress, 1993), 172–93.

19. Walter Wink, *Engaging the Powers* (Minneapolis: Fortress, 1992), 101. Because of our emphasis on community ministry as standing on the wall between the political and the religious, we hear with interest Wink's contention that the domination system is both a political and spiritual state of being—part of the meaning of Satan as an embodiment

of the domination system. "The dominator exerts power by extracting being from the dominated. Capitalists often get more than the power and surplus value of their workers; they also degrade the workers' being and puff up their own being. Thus, the unmistakable narcissism of class superiority. White racists do more than materially exploit blacks; they make themselves members of a superior race and regard blacks as less than human, even animalistic. Sexually exploitative males do more than control the labor and bodies of women; they make themselves into the bearers of rationality and history, while the woman is made into dumb nature. Thus domination always entails more than injustice. It wounds — and it intends to wound — the very soul itself."

20. That which Wink calls the myth of redemptive violence inundates our popular culture. The myth may be traced to the Babylonian "Enuma Elish" of around 1250 BCE, which puts the creation of the world in a context of extreme violence. "The implications are clear: humanity is created from the blood of a murdered god. Our very origin is violent. Killing is in our blood. Humanity is not the originator of evil, but merely finds evil already present and perpetuates it.... War, conquest, plunder, rape, and enslavement are all ordained in the very constitution of the universe, which itself is formed from the corpse of a murdered goddess. 'Civilization' is a condition of periodic or perpetual warfare, 'peace' the achievement of warfare, 'prosperity' the fruit of warfare successfully accomplished" (ibid., 65–57).

21. In her reflection on the text, "A stranger you must not oppress, you yourselves know the heart of a stranger, for you were strangers in the land of Egypt" (Exod. 23:9), Johanna Bos observes: "For ancient Israel, the recall of past experience served on the one hand to determine appropriate treatment of the stranger. Furthermore, this type of recall sought to locate the identity of the covenant community in its experience of suffering. The self understanding of the community thus depended for a great deal on its ability to recognize and name its suffering.... The stranger will not be excluded from the community insofar as the community is able to name its own experience of exclusion. Rather than pushing this experience to the margin, the call is to acknowledge it as a mark of identification for the alternative community. By implication the text calls the community to become strangers in the land of Egypt" (Johanna W. H. Bos, "Solidarity with the Stranger," in *A Journey to Justice* [Louisville: Presbyterian Committee on the Self-Development of Peoples, Presbyterian Church (USA), 1993], 51).

22. Wink, *Engaging the Powers*, 66–67.

23. Ibid., 67.

24. No one is more sensitive or more eloquent on the implication of the faith community in the general failings of institutional structures than Philip Potter, the former general secretary of the World Council

of Churches: "But it was not until the 1970s that we were forced beyond generalities to face the real issues of the ecumenical sharing of resources. A series of events made this clear. The first reality was that the development aid resulted in the rich countries getting richer and the poor countries getting poorer. As we noted earlier this is a consequence of entrenched economic and political structures in both the giving and receiving countries, maintained through the trans-national corporations and the growing militarization of society in a large number of countries of the world. What is true of governments and industrial enterprises is also true for the churches. Their structures of giving and receiving do not facilitate real partnership. Good will and fine statements are not enough to overcome the impediment: what is required is rigorous examination of these structures. Second, the issues of dominance and dependence, or power and powerlessness, have become clearer in recent years. The churches of the rich countries continue to insist on bilateral relationships over against multilateral ecumenical ones, just as governments and corporations do. The response of this uncovering of dominance and dependence is that the poorer people have to learn the meaning and the means of gaining power. The issue has therefore become empowering the powerless. The initiatives have to be taken by the poor themselves" (Phillip Potter, *Life in All Its Fullness* [Grand Rapids, Mich.: Eerdmans, 1982], 115–16).

25. Ibid., 171–72.

26. Karen Armstrong, *The Battle for God* (New York: Alfred A. Knopf, 2000).

27. From an unpublished interview with the author.

28. In conjunction with the argument of the previous section, it should be noted that, as a result of these various cooperative efforts, Texas became a model for state-based ecumenical relations between Catholics and Protestants (the Texas Conference of Churches), and Houston became a model for interfaith relations (Interfaith Ministries of Greater Houston).

29. Bellah postulated that forms of religion other than those that are direct descendants of the American Puritans would pick up the torch to reestablish a responsible balance between individualism and a common sociopolitical culture with common commitments. "Much that is happening [in the religious ferment of the 1960s and 1970s] can be understood in terms of the Protestant conversion/covenant pattern — even when it does not use that language. But there is a renewal of the sources of religious imagination that have been dry for two centuries. Most of that renewal has come from outside the Protestant tradition — from the oriental emphasis on immediate experience and harmony with nature, from the Catholic emphasis on community and sacramental life, from the Jewish experience of keeping the faith in the midst of disaster. But the millennial note, the ethical criticism of society, and the insistence on

the role of a remnant that already embodies the future, are thoroughly in consonance with the central theme of the American Protestant experience" (Robert Bellah, *The Broken Covenant: American Civil Religion in a Time of Trial* [New York: Seabury, 1975], 158).

30. "Interfaith Relations and the Churches" (New York: National Council of Churches, 1999), Recommendations 9 and 10.

31. In her article "Resistance and the Transformation of Human Experience," Ellen Wondra suggests that there are certain qualities of authentic relationship that by themselves bespeak both resistance and transformation. She says that one example would be the manner in which we relate to each other as people of different faith commitments uniting for the sake of our community to become more like the community that God intends for it to be. (Wondra in *New Visions for the Americas*, 150.)

32. Juan Luis Segundo, *The Liberation of Theology* (Maryknoll, N.Y.: Orbis Books, 1976), 44. Segundo puts "service of reconciliation" in quotes because he wants to oppose a reading of 2 Corinthians 5:19 ("God was in Christ reconciling the world to himself.") or Colossians 1:19–20 ("For in him all the fullness of God was pleased to dwell, and through him to reconcile to himself all things . . . ") that would slide over the liberation of humanity as penultimate to the reconciliation of all things.

33. Mark Heim's trinitarian basis for interreligious understanding presents essentially the same problem for interfaith and ecumenical community ministry as the christological one. I have no quarrel with his "more pluralistic hypothesis," which he calls "orientational pluralism" nor the admission of "multiple religious ends," which may indeed lead to a greater sense of respect for the faith of the other. What I find unfortunate is Heim's insistence that the meeting of any two or various faiths, no matter on which plane, must be predicated on their uniqueness. Thus, in regard to Christian ecumenism he claims: "The historical modes of Christian confession are the only voices through which broader Christian unity can be affirmed and validated" (*Salvations* [Maryknoll, N.Y.: Orbis Books, 1995], 184). In community ministry we learn that statements such as this may not, in fact, be true, and that they may only serve to promote competition over cooperation.

4. From Local to Global and Back

1. Gary Gunderson, *Deeply Woven Roots* (Minneapolis: Fortress, 1997), 54.

2. L. A. Hoedemaker, "Naming the World in the Name of the Coming One: Changing Relations between Mission, Modernity and Eschatology," *Exchange* (Leiden, Brill) 27, no. 3 (1998), 203.

3. The ethicist Larry Rasmussen, an exponent of the term "sustainable community" (as opposed to "sustainable development"), says: "Sustainable community works on the principle of subsidiarity and asks

how you wrap both economy and environment around local communities and bio-regions. In contrast to the ways of globalization as current corporate capitalism, even 'greened,' sustainable community tries to preserve or create such as the following: greater economic self-sufficiency locally and regionally, with a view to the bio-regions themselves as basic to human organization; agriculture appropriate to regions and in the hands of local owners and workers using local knowledge and crop varieties, with ability to save their own seeds, treat their own plants and soils with their own products; the preservation of local and regional traditions, language and cultures and a resistance to global homogenization of culture and values; a revival of religious life and a sense of the sacred vis-à-vis a present way of life that leeches the sacred from the everyday and has no sense of mystery because it reduces life to the utilitarian" (Larry Rasmussen, "The Earth Charter and Christian Social Ethics," unpublished paper, 2001, 9–10). The list goes on but I have quoted that portion which pertains especially to the local community, including the last phrase, out of my conviction that revival of religious life begins at the local level and the embedded unity of congregations there.

4. Larry Rasmussen, *Moral Fragments and Moral Community* (Minneapolis: Fortress, 1993), 10.

5. Ellen van Wolde, *Stories of the Beginning* (London: SCM Press, 1996).

6. Ibid., 118.

7. Ibid., 127.

8. Ibid., 130.

9. Ibid., 132.

10. See the Web site earthcharter.org.

11. In this debate, "regional" should perhaps not receive quite the bad press that I have given it here. For one thing, as Rasmussen points out (above), the problem of preserving earth's biodiversity might best be approached on a regional basis. Furthermore, although globalization defines local in terms of regionalization, a region may also become an arena for mobilizing localities against the worst abuses of globalization. If localities have any hope of maintaining their integrity in the face of the global juggernaut, a certain degree of accommodation to the concept of a region might be called for. The region is the playing field (albeit not a level one) where the forces of globalization and local self-determination meet.

12. Lukas Vischer, "How Sustainable Is the Present Project of World Trade?" in *Sustainability and Globalization,* ed. Julio de Santa Ana (Geneva: WCC, 1998).

13. Charles W. Rawlings, "The Global Economy's Opening Hand: The Steel Shut Down," in *A Tapestry of Justice, Service, and Unity,* ed. Arleon L. Kelley (Tacoma, Wash.: National Association of Ecumenical and Interreligious Staff Press, 2004), 180.

14. Vischer, "How Sustainable Is the Present Project of World Trade?" 48.

15. Ibid., 53–54.

16. Robert Bellah, *The Broken Covenant: American Civil Religion in a Time of Trial* (New York: Seabury, 1975), 23. Bellah cites Jefferson's second inaugural address: "I need, too, the favor of the Being in whose hands we are, who led our forefathers, as Israel of old, from their native land, and planted them in a country with all the necessities and comforts of life."

17. In "Reclaiming Motherhood: A Search for an Eco-Feminist Vision," in *Sustainability and Globalization*, ed. de Santa Ana, 135–36, Gnanadason reflects on the experience of women in particular in India and how government decisions relative to "development" have tended to break their ties with the earth and their local community. She cites the destruction of an indigenous Bonda community by the construction of an aluminum factory in the middle of their forest lands. She relates stories of women working in relatively close proximity to the resources of the earth in a nation that is losing 1.3 million hectares of forests each year, with 56.6 percent of its land being eroded by water and wind, and with its groundwater reserves falling rapidly. She deplores the notion that development and economic growth might be a panacea, because this ideology is implicated in breaking the link with Mother Earth and in pushing hundreds of millions of people ever deeper into poverty. She agrees that this situation presents a challenge and an opportunity for those with ecumenical commitments, and she derives hope from Larry Rasmussen's vision of the ecumenical earth where local and particular communities live in close harmony with the earth. Many there are who are beginning to make these connections — between theology and relationships, politics and resistance, earth and community, and between globalization and intensified competition, which is destructive of all these connections. In his essay, "Demystifying the Single Thought and Single Structure," Joannes Petrou speaks of quality of life and relationships as a "criterion for a sustainable society." He points out the inherent weakness of projecting competition as a value when, in the context of globalization, it works against the values of solidarity, mutuality, and cooperation. He calls for "a different way of understanding reality," one that is "diametrically opposed to the conception of life based on economic productivity and the individualistic achievement of power and prosperity" (in *Sustainability and Globalization*, ed. de Santa Ana, 129).

18. The Institute for Democracy Studies has documented the impact of such funds on one denomination (Presbyterian Church [USA]). See the book by Lewis C. Daly, *A Moment to Decide: The Crisis in Mainstream Presbyterianism* (New York: Institute for Democracy Studies, 1999). The well-funded, successful ten-year project to claim the Southern Baptist

Convention and its immense network of affiliated institutions for an activist Falwellian social agenda is another case in point.

19. Boer was a missionary of the (conservative Calvinist) Christian Reformed Church, who, while based in Nigeria, was radicalized by the policies and actions of TNCs there. His book *Caught in the Middle: Christians in Transnational Corporations* (Jos, Nigeria: Institute of Church and Society, 1992), describes both the destructive actions of TNCs in the developing world and the implication of most North American Christians through individual and corporate (including denominational) investment practices. The chapter cited is found on pp. 80–98.

20. See the article, "Is a Sustainable Society Possible in the Context of Globalization?" in *Sustainability and Globalization*, ed. de Santa Ana, 15–16.

21. Paul D. Hanson, *The People Called* (San Francisco: Harper & Row, 1986), 511.

22. Ibid., 515.

23. "Religious Men and Women in Latin America Today," in *Mission in the Third Millennium*, ed. Robert J. Schreiter (Maryknoll, N.Y.: Orbis Books, 2001), 100–101.

24. Schreiter, "Epilogue," ibid., 150–51.

25. Anthony Giddens, *Runaway World* (New York: Routledge, 2000), 24–37. Giddens sees globalization as a chaotic process, which still may be ours to shape.

26. Roland Robertson, "Glocalization," in *Global Modernities*, ed. Mike Featherstone, Scott Lash, and Roland Robertson (London: Sage Publications, 1995), 25–41. Although he is persuasive in arguing against the idea that globalization necessarily homogenizes life, it should be noted that he does not deal with the political problem of overriding or trivializing local participatory democracy and the long-term effects of that on local cultures. Nevertheless it may be both helpful and hopeful for us to entertain the notion of a given, structural give-and-take between local and global culture: "Globalization — in the broadest sense, the compression of the world — has involved and increasingly involves the creation and the incorporation of locality, processes, which themselves largely shape, in turn, the compression of the world" (40).

27. Larry Rasmussen, *Earth Community, Earth Ethics* (Maryknoll, N.Y.: Orbis Books, 1996), 337. In this respect, Rasmussen takes his cue from the papal encyclical *Quadragesimo anno* (1931), which he quotes: "It is an injustice and at the same time a grave evil and disturbance of right order to assign to a greater and higher association what lesser and subordinate organizations can do" (footnote, 336).

5. Toward the Beloved Community

1. It is no accident that covenant theory developed simultaneously as both theological and political theory — both heavily influenced by a

common source — Heinrich Bullinger's *A Brief Exposition of the One and Eternal Testament or Covenant of God*, in which love of God referred to religious practice and love of neighbor referred to political processes, with the two inextricably intertwined. On Bullinger and his influence on political, theological, and political/theological thinkers, the author is indebted to Charles S. McCoy and J. Wayne Baker, *Fountainhead of Federalism: Heinrich Bullinger and the Covenantal Tradition* (Louisville: Westminster/John Knox, 1991). This book includes a translation of Bullinger's "De testamento seu feodere Dei unico et aeterno" (1534).

2. Buffalo and Rochester, New York, are two of several communities that have enacted local Living Wage laws. Louisville and Lexington, Kentucky, are two of the more recent cities to enact local fairness legislation.

3. In the work *Politics,* published in 1603, the founding theoretician of covenantal politics, Johannes Althusius, says, " 'Politics' is the art of linking humans together in order to establish, develop, and conserve social life among them. . . . The content of politics, therefore, is association, in which the symbiotes make covenant with one another, either explicitly or tacitly, to a mutual sharing of whatever things are useful and necessary for harmony and productive activity in social life" (*Politics* 1:1–2, quoted in McCoy and Baker, *Fountainhead of Federalism,* 55). Brueggemann says that the marks of covenant community reflect "a subversive ecclesiology in deep conflict with our conventions." He contrasts covenant community with communities of fate where we have no choice and those of convenience in which we have no serious interest. "Against both of those, we are to have a called community — not a voluntary association but a people addressed and bound in a concrete and abiding loyalty" (Walter Brueggemann, *A Social Reading of the Old Testament,* ed. Patrick Miller [Minneapolis: Fortress, 1994], 50).

One reason for the development of covenant theory was its usefulness to Althusius and others in opposition to political theorist Jean Bodin (1530–96), who defended the divine right of kings, centralized absolutism, and opposed the notion that there could be any justified resistance to established political authority.

Althusius's writings followed upon an earlier, tractarian use of covenantal thought by Philippe Duplessis-Mornay, who had anonymously published a tract entitled "A Defense of Liberty Against Tyrants" (1579). In it he justified resistance against tyrants based on the idea that society implied a series of religious and political covenants, making the civil rulers responsible both to God and to the people, who were the locus of civil authority. Mornay asserted that the ruler could be deposed if he did not keep his covenant with God and the people (McCoy and Baker, *Fountainhead of Federalism,* 47–49). (The alliance formed in Fairhope, Alabama [above], owes a debt to Mornay, Althusius, et al.) Covenantal political theory, as enunciated by Mornay and articulated and developed by Althusius was, among other things, a theological justification for political resistance. Mornay made a point that carries down to our perspective on community ministry today, namely, that: "God had made a covenant with the entire community, with the people under the rule of the king. The king and the people as a corporate body acting as a single entity had obligated themselves within this covenant. It was the king's covenanted responsibility to ensure that the people kept the covenant. It was the covenanted responsibility of the people to see that the king kept the covenant" (McCoy and Baker, *Fountainhead of Federalism*, 33–34). The authors trace the influence of Althusius on James Madison, via his teacher John Witherspoon, clergy signer of the Declaration of Independence and president of the College of New Jersey (Princeton). Witherspoon learned covenant politics/theology at the University of Edinburgh, which had arrived there *via* England, the United Provinces of the Netherlands, Germany, and ultimately, Switzerland and Bullinger.

For us today this theory means that in a local community, the people as a whole, and the processes by which each element upholds its particular responsibility determine the character of the community. However rarely, these local initiatives might eventually have a resisting impact on regional configurations and national/global policy.

4. Charles Winquist in *Desiring Theology* (Chicago: University of Chicago Press, 1995) speaks of a "secular mandate for theology." He cites a need that theological discourse can fulfill of a "radical critique that reveals how much we must care for the other." It makes for the "possibility for meaningful community." He calls theological thinking a "deconstructive force" that is a "continuous pressure against the totalization and closure of a dominant discourse." Thus, when local congregations combine their embedded unity, their social position, and their inclusive theological language of the covenant, they bring a gift of great value to the body politic — a "radical critique that is practiced in the belief that life is less beautiful when people are oppressed and disenfranchised, when nature is exploited and despoiled, and when the diverse singularities of life are denied recognition and exfoliation" (Winquist, *Desiring Theology*, 143–46). Winquist calls this deconstructive religious discourse "paraethics," which corresponds to my view of the role of the local religious community as it relates to the body politic on the basis of covenantal constructs.

5. David Baak, "Reflections on the History of the Grand Rapids Center for Ecumenism," in *Tapestry of Justice, Service and Unity*, ed. Arleon L. Kelley (Tacoma, Wash.: National Association of Ecumenical and Interreligious Staff Press, 2004), 240–60, and in telephone interview with the author on August 30, 2001.

6. *Powerful Whispers: The Report of the Bradford Hearings* (Bradford, U.K.: Bradford Metropolitan Faith in the City Forum, 1995), 9.

The Introduction states that the purpose is "to stimulate a public debate . . . about the ways in which we want to live together, and the sort of future we want to build for our children and grandchildren."

7. I reiterate that no religious community is inclusive enough to embrace the scope of God's covenant by itself. This is exactly why covenant was and is a subject for political theorists and social critics as well as for theologians. In any case, the powerful scriptural mandate given to religious communities to care and advocate for the poor could never be fully implemented by a single religious community. By way of illustration, the feminist scholar Eleanor Haney loved her Beacon Street United Church of Christ, and she experienced a spirit of transformation with a strong sense of community there (Eleanor Haney, *The Great Commandment* [Cleveland, Pilgrim, 1988], 25). It was a "community of discipleship" but it was also a "community in alliance with others." Small groups of members worked in alliance with members of the wider community to address racism in the local community, work on local issues related to economic justice, sew infant clothes for an ecumenical aid group, aid in the development of alternative treatment and healing processes in the field of mental health, establish a shelter for battered women in the area, and meet with representatives of all local interested groups to discuss how social and ecological issues are intertwined (28). A covenant of membership included an acknowledgment of the new member's ecosocial location and the implications for the person's life in the community (32). This is a description of covenant theology in action; clearly, as "beloved" as the gathered religious community may be, the appellation "beloved community" belongs to those processes in which this congregation and others are engaged for the betterment of the local body politic: "Only as we become part of the ongoing struggle for justice, sustainability and well-being in concert with others, particularly with those who are different from ourselves, will our hearts continue to open. God speaks to us concretely through the voices of all her people, plants, and animals" (36). Nor is the beloved community an ideal community, or a matter of some places being invested by God with more significance than others. In every place we encounter a "dominant community" of which we may be a part, or which may be part of our thinking. The dominant community is a community of death. It is governed by an inner, driving force that is ultimately one of oppression and destruction. It may from time to time present a façade of sunny pleasantness and placid uneventfulness, but underneath lay the Holocaust and the holocausts, the ethnic cleansing and Hiroshima, injustice and violence of every kind, and persistent racism. Authentic ecumenical and interfaith community ministry acknowledges that this reality is the backdrop and foil for all of its operations. Although it looks to the local as a source of revelation, this is no romantic view. As Winquist says, "Theology is a work against the disappointment of thinking." The scriptures, moreover, do not gloss over the grim reality of the

domination system, which is precisely what makes their affirmative witness important for us. Beginning with the covenant with Noah and the sign of the rainbow, they form the basis for a beloved community. This spirit is akin to that which pervades the Adrienne Rich poem: "My heart is moved by all I cannot save / So much has been destroyed / I have to cast my lot with those / who age after age, perversely, / with no extraordinary power, / reconstitute the world" ("Natural Resources," in *The Dream of a Common Language: Poems 1974–77* [New York: W. W. Norton, 1978], 66–67). Based on all the above listed in no particular order, here are some aspects of a sober hope that community ministry may attempt to bring:

> For the revealing of embedded unity among faith groups
> For acknowledgment and respect for diversity and difference
> For sustainability based on local resources and talents
> For participatory political processes and leadership development
> For mutually supportive contacts with other communities
> For the power of self-determination — to resist dictation by outside forces
> For a nurturing culture that promotes the general welfare
> For respect for sustaining and beautiful earthly environments
> For a sense of accountability to a higher power/standard that also sustains
> For a spirit of hospitality to the stranger and to the neighbor in need
> For honest self-criticism and the admission of need for improvement
> For an awareness of economic forces of global destruction and oppression
> IN SUM: For a radical critique of and resistance to the dominant culture.

8. Sharon Welch, *Communities of Resistance and Solidarity* (Maryknoll, N.Y.: Orbis Books, 1985), 90.

9. In the view of Miroslav Volf, the hope of a covenantal way of thinking is that it is covenantal rather than contractual: "Precisely because covenant is lasting, the parties themselves cannot be conceived as individuals whose identities are external to one another and who are related to one another only by virtue of their moral will and moral practice. Rather, the very identity of each is formed through relation to others" (Miroslav Volf, *Exclusion and Embrace* [Nashville: Abingdon, 1996], 154).

10. Ibid., 153.

11. Such a demonstration may, by itself, be a source of hope in a local community. Richard Niebuhr, on the subject of religious freedom, asks whether such a freedom can be maintained on the basis of tolerating one another. "Or does it presuppose the presence of a sense of responsibility

to a cause that goes beyond all limited causes and [the people's] acceptance of explicit loyalty to a community of faithfulness that is eternal and inclusive?" (H. Richard Niebuhr, "The Idea of Covenant and American Democracy," *Church History* 23 [June 1954]: 132). By raising the issue of religious freedom in relation to the notion of covenant, Niebuhr signified the centrality of this theological/political idea in the development of participatory democracy. He also used and underlined one meaning of a word often employed in this book — resistance. Religious unity, for example, is the beginning of resistance in the body politic precisely because it presupposes par excellence "the presence of a sense of responsibility to a cause that goes beyond all limited causes."

12. "Free is whoever claims the right of resistance," says Jürgen Moltmann ("Covenant or Leviathan? Political Theology for Modern Times" *Scottish Journal of Theology* 47, no. 1 [1994]: 20).

13. Welch, *Communities of Resistance and Solidarity*, 40–41.

14. Welch comments on and quotes James Cone on the importance of liberating memories: "James Cone describes the liberating impact of Christianity on African-American women and men during and after slavery. He states that the religion of a God who affirms the worth of all people was lived despite the ideological interpretations of that religion by those who supported slavery. The black church was the locus of experiences of acceptance, love and dignity. The power that comes from believing that 'God' (that which is ultimate) affirms the importance and value of the lives of slaves prevented black acquiescence to the definition of themselves as sub-human by white slave owners. The record shows clearly that black slaves believed that just as God had delivered Moses and the Israelites from Egyptian bondage, God will deliver black people from American slavery" (ibid., 41, citing James Cone, *God of the Oppressed* [New York: Seabury Press, 1975], 11).

15. Gustavo Gutiérrez, *A Theology of Liberation* (Maryknoll, N.Y.: Orbis Books, 1973), 204–5.

16. Rosemary Ruether once envisioned a localized institutional framework informed by these ideas. It included a high degree of communalization — especially in regard to child raising and household administration. She advocated a decentralized economy. She proposed greater political autonomy of local communities and a close, conscious connection of each community with Earth: "Since local communities would make many of the decisions that effect their immediate lives, self-government would counteract much of the present sense of alienation and powerlessness of the atomized individual. Such solidarity is not utopian, but eminently practical, pointing to our actual solidarity with all others and with our mother, the earth, which is the actual ground of our being" (Rosemary Ruether, *New Woman, New Earth* [Boston: Beacon Press, 1995], 208–11).

17. See the Interfaith Hospitality Network Web site. Stressing the crucial importance of local interfaith and ecumenical coalitions as we do does

not preclude the use of certain national networks, provided the ministry takes its cues from the local community.

18. This project contrasts with a typical Habitat for Humanity project in the following ways: (1) The HFH projects tend to be built exclusively in poor neighborhoods where they do not challenge race- and class-based segregated housing patterns. (2) The above is the case partly because HFH in principle does not use governmental programs that are set up precisely for the purpose of promoting affordable housing, thus devaluing the role of government in this important field. (3) HFH relies on volunteers from churches in a purely utilitarian fashion—that is, there is no theological basis given for working together across denominational or faith lines. (4) In fact, HFH is exclusively Christian in its charter and pretends that there is such a thing as "Christian economics," which they follow in their housing construction programs. (5) Although HFH has local chapters, it follows a tried-and-true national formula that allows very little variation from locale to locale.

19. Whether in Leviticus or in Jesus' parable of the Good Samaritan (Luke 10:25–37), we find a conflation in the scriptures of the terms "neighbor" and "stranger." One of the ethical guidelines that may be inferred from these texts is that of hospitality to the stranger—the stranger being anyone from whom we feel separated because of his or her "otherness." That otherness may be based on poverty or disability as much as on cultural or physical difference. The love that humanity owes God binds humanity together by virtue of God's compassionate covenant with all of creation, including humanity. That promise makes every stranger a neighbor in and with our common home, Earth.

Selected Bibliography

Included here are works that contribute significantly to an understanding of the genesis of the interfaith and ecumenical ministry movement or that have here served as background for a theology of such.

Albrecht, Gloria. *The Character of Our Communities: Toward an Ethic of Liberation for the Church.* Nashville: Abingdon, 1995.

Bellah, Robert. *The Broken Covenant: American Civil Religion in a Time of Trial.* New York: Seabury, 1975.

———. *Habits of the Heart.* Chicago: University of Chicago Press, 1992.

———. *Uncivil Religion.* New York: Crossroad, 1987.

Bonhoeffer, Dietrich. *Life Together.* New York: Harper, 1954.

Brueggemann, Walter. *The Covenanted Self.* Minneapolis: Fortress, 1999.

———. *Interpretation and Obedience.* Minneapolis: Fortress, 1991.

Buber, Martin. *I and Thou.* Edinburgh: T. & T. Clark, 1937.

Cone, James. *A Black Theology of Liberation.* Maryknoll, N.Y.: Orbis Books, 1986.

de Santa Ana, Julio, ed. *Sustainability and Globalization.* Geneva: World Council of Churches, 1998.

Diehl, William, *Christianity and Real Life.* Philadelphia: Fortress, 1986.

Dupuis, Jacques. *Toward a Christian Theology of Religious Pluralism.* Maryknoll, N.Y.: Orbis Books, 1997.

Elazar, Daniel Judah. *The Covenant Tradition in Politics.* 4 vols. New Brunswick, N.J.: Transaction Publishers, 1995–98.

Fackenheim, Emil. *To Mend the World.* New York: Schocken Books, 1984.

Gardner, Clinton E. *The Church as a Prophetic Community.* Philadelphia: Westminster, 1967.

Giddens, Anthony. *Runaway World.* New York: Routledge, 2000.

Glennon, Frederick E., Gary S. Hauk, and Darryl M. Trimiew, eds. *Living Responsibly in Community.* Lanham, Md.: University Press of America, 1997.

Goudszwaard, Robert. *Globalization and the Kingdom of God.* Grand Rapids, Mich.: Baker Books, 2001.

Gunderson, Gary. *Deeply Woven Roots.* Minneapolis: Fortress, 1997.

Gutiérrez, Gustavo. *A Theology of Liberation.* Maryknoll, N.Y.: Orbis Books, 1973.

Hall, Cameron. *Lay Action: The Church's Third Force.* New York: Friendship Press, 1974.

Haney, Eleanor. *The Great Commandment.* Cleveland: Pilgrim, 1998.

Hanson, Paul D. *The People Called.* San Francisco: Harper & Row, 1986.

Hessel, Dieter T. *Social Ministry.* Philadelphia: Westminster, 1982.

Hick, John. *God Has Many Names.* Philadelphia: Westminster, 1982.

Hoedemaker, L. A. "Naming the World in the Name of the Coming One: Changing Relations between Mission, Modernity and Eschatology." *Exchange* (Leiden, Brill) 27, no. 3 (1998).

Hopewell, James F. *Congregation: Stories and Structures.* Edited by Barbara G. Wheeler. Philadelphia: Fortress, 1987.

Korten, David C. *When Corporations Rule the World.* West Hartford, Conn.: Kumarian, 1998.

Kraemer, Hendrik *A Theology of the Laity.* Philadelphia: Westminster, 1958.

Lévinas, Emmanuel. *Of God Who Comes to Mind.* Stanford, Calif.: Stanford University Press, 1998.

Lincoln, C. Eric, and Lawrence H. Mamiya. *The Black Church in the African American Experience.* Durham, N.C.: Duke University Press, 1990.

May, William E. *Becoming Human.* Dayton, Ohio: Pflaum Publishing, 1975.

McCoy, Charles S., and J. Wayne Baker. *Fountainhead of Federalism: Heinrich Bullinger and the Covenantal Tradition.* Louisville: Westminster/John Knox, 1991.

Miller, Perry. *The American Puritans.* New York: Anchor Books, 1956.

Moltmann, Jürgen. "Covenant or Leviathan? Political Theology for Modern Times." *Scottish Journal of Theology* 47, no. 1 (1994).

Mount, Eric. *Covenant, Community and Common Good.* Cleveland: Pilgrim, 1999.

Nelson, C. Ellis. *Congregations: Their Power to Form and Transform.* Atlanta: John Knox, 1988.

Niebuhr, H. Richard. *Faith on Earth.* New Haven, Conn.: Yale University Press, 1989.

———. "The Idea of Covenant and American Democracy." *Church History* 23 (June 1954).

———. *The Responsible Self.* New York: Harper & Row, 1963.

———. *The Social Sources of Denominationalism.* New York: H. Holt and Co., 1929.

O'Connor, Elizabeth. *The New Community*. New York: Harper & Row, 1976.

Paris, Peter. *The Social Teaching of the Black Churches*. Minneapolis: Fortress, 1985.

———. *The Spirituality of African Peoples*. Minneapolis: Fortress, 1995.

Peck, George, and John F. Hofman, eds. *The Laity in Ministry*. Valley Forge, Pa.: Judson, 1984.

Potter, Philip. *Life in All Its Fullness*. Grand Rapids, Mich.: Eerdmans, 1982.

Powerful Whispers: The Report of the Bradford Hearings. Bradford, England: Bradford Metropolitan Faith in the City Forum, 1995.

Raisor, Conrad. *Ecumenism in Transition*. Geneva: World Council of Churches, 1991.

Rasmussen, Larry. "The Earth Charter and Christian Social Ethics," unpublished paper.

———. *Earth Community, Earth Ethics*. Maryknoll, N.Y.: Orbis Books, 1996.

———. *Give Us Word of the Humankind We Left to Thee: Dietrich Bonhoeffer — His Significance for North Americans*. Minneapolis: Fortress, 1990.

———. *Moral Fragments and Moral Community*. Minneapolis: Fortress, 1993.

Reitz, Rudiger. *The Church in Experiment*. Nashville: Abingdon, 1969.

Rose, Steve. *The Grass Roots Church*. New York: Holt, Rinehart and Winston, 1966.

Royce, Josiah. *The Problem of Christianity*. Chicago: University of Chicago, Press, 1968 [1918].

Ruether, Rosemary. *Gaia and God*. San Francisco: Harper, 1992.

Sawyer, Mary R. *Black Ecumenism*. Valley Forge, Pa.: Trinity Press International, 1994.

Segundo, Juan Luis. *The Liberation of Theology*. Maryknoll, N.Y.: Orbis Books, 1976.

Shaull, Richard. *The Reformation and Liberation Theology*. Louisville: Westminster/John Knox, 1991.

Shaull, Richard, and Gustavo Gutiérrez. *Liberation and Change*. Atlanta: John Knox, 1977.

van der Bent, Ans. *Commitment to God's World*. Geneva: World Council of Churches, 1995.

van Wijk-Bos, Johanna W. H. "Solidarity with the Stranger." In *A Journey to Justice*. Louisville: Presbyterian Committee on the Self-Development of Peoples, Presbyterian Church (USA), 1993.

van Wolde, Ellen. *Stories of the Beginning*. London: SCM Press, 1996.

Webber, George W. *The Congregation in Mission*. New York: Abingdon, 1964.

Welch, Sharon. *Communities of Resistance and Solidarity.* Maryknoll, N.Y.: Orbis Books, 1985.
————. *A Feminist Ethic of Risk.* Minneapolis: Fortress, 1990.
Williams, Colin. *What in the World.* New York: National Council of Churches, 1964.
————. *Where in the World.* New York: National Council of Churches, 1963.
Wink, Walter. *Engaging the Powers.* Minneapolis: Fortress, 1992.
Winquist, Charles. *Desiring Theology.* Chicago: University of Chicago Press, 1995.
Wuthnow, Robert. *Acts of Compassion.* Princeton, N.J.: Princeton University Press, 1991.

By the Author

"Community Ministry: The Establishment of Ecumenical Local Mission in North American Church Life." *Journal of Ecumenical Studies* 22, no. 1 (Winter 1985).
"Community Ministry: The Wild Card in Ecumenical Relations and Social Ministry." *Journal of Ecumenical Studies* 25, no. 4 (Fall 1988).
A Practical Guide to Community Ministry. Louisville: Westminster/John Knox, 1993.
"A Personal Perspective on the Community Ministry Movement." *Journal of Ecumenical Studies* 35, no. 2 (Spring 1998).
"The Founding of Smith Haven Ministries." In *A Tapestry of Justice, Service and Unity,* Edited by Arleon L. Kelley. Tacoma, Wash.: National Association of Ecumenical and Interreligious Staff, 2004.
"The Self-Discovery of Texas Ecumenism as a Counter-Cultural Movement." In *A Tapestry of Justice, Service and Unity.* Edited by Arleon L. Kelley. Tacoma, Wash.: National Association of Ecumenical and Interreligious Staff, 2004.

Index

HEBREW BIBLE

NEW TESTAMENT